I tried to comfort Willie. "Take courage. Brighter days will come."

"No they won't," he said. "We'll have to stay here forever. We'll never be free."

"We're growing older and stronger. Soon we might be allowed to earn some money of our own. Before long we might have enough money to buy our freedom."

"I don't think so. Besides, we shouldn't *have* to buy our freedom. No one has the right to own anyone else."

## A Background Note about the Book

*Incidents in the Life of a Slave Girl* is a true story, written by a young woman who was born into slavery in 1813. At that time, farmers in the Southern "Slave States" depended on slave labor. Because slave owners had paid cash for their slaves, Southern laws allowed the masters and mistresses to do whatever they wanted with their slaves—even rape or kill them. And since slaves were considered property, not human beings, many white people saw no contradiction between owning slaves and being "good Christians."

If slaves did not obey their masters, they were beaten, jailed, sold away from their families, or killed. Occasionally, owners freed their slaves or allowed slaves to buy their own freedom. But even free black people did not have the same rights as white citizens. In desperation, some slaves ran away to the Northern "Free States," where people were not allowed to own other human beings.

How could a young slave woman free herself from the horrors of slavery? Slaves had no rights. They could not marry, raise their own children, or even protect themselves from moral or physical harm. But as Harriet Jacobs grows from a slave girl to a free woman, she finds ways to preserve her human dignity. She protects herself sometimes by speaking out and sometimes by remaining silent. Writing her story was Harriet's ultimate act of self-assertion.

# Harriet Jacobs

# Incidents in the Life of a Slave Girl

*****

*Written by Herself*

Edited, and with an Afterword,
by Lisa Barsky

 **THE TOWNSEND LIBRARY**

# INCIDENTS IN THE
# LIFE OF A SLAVE GIRL

**TP** THE TOWNSEND LIBRARY

For more titles in the Townsend Library,
visit our website: **www.townsendpress.com**

All new material in this edition is
copyright © 2004 by Townsend Press.
Printed in the United States of America

0 9 8 7 6

Illustrations © 2004 by Hal Taylor

**Townsend Press, Inc.**
**439 Kelley Drive**
**West Berlin, New Jersey 080911**

ISBN-13: 978-1-59194-026-5
ISBN-10: 1-59194-026-5

Library of Congress Control Number:
2003116571

# TABLE OF CONTENTS

# CHAPTER 1

I was born a slave. The year was 1813; the place, the coastal town of Edenton, North Carolina. The first six years of my life were happy, partly because my parents concealed from me that I was a slave.

My grandmothers were slaves, and my grandfathers were the white men who owned them. My parents were owned by different people, but their owners allowed them to live together in a comfortable home and to take care of my brother William and me. Willie was two years younger than I.

My father was an intelligent, skilled carpenter. His owner, Mrs. Jacobs, allowed him to earn his own money, but he had to support his family and pay Mrs. Jacobs $200 a year. People hired him to supervise building construction. Father wanted to buy Willie and me from Mrs. Jacobs. He kept offering her all his hard-earned money, but she never agreed.

Edenton's residents called my maternal grandmother "Aunt Martha." She was the

1

daughter of a white man and a slave whom he owned. Upon the death of her father, Grandmother was freed. But on her way to live with some relatives, she was captured and sold to new owners, Mr. and Mrs. Nash. The Nashes found that Grandmother was intelligent, faithful, and useful: a valuable piece of property.

Mr. Nash was my mother's father. Three months after my mother was born, Mrs. Nash had a daughter, Ruth. Grandmother had to wean her own baby so that she could breast-feed Ruth. As children, my mother and Ruth played together and were almost like sisters.

Grandmother baked delicious cakes and crackers that everyone wanted to buy. She asked Mrs. Nash if she could bake them at night, after she had finished her chores. Mrs. Nash gave her permission, provided that Grandmother paid for her own clothing and her children's clothing. Each year, Grandmother set aside some money, so that someday she could buy her children.

When Mr. Nash died, Mrs. Nash kept Grandmother as her slave. My mother and three of her siblings each went to one of the Nashes' four children. (Each heir wanted an equal portion of Mr. Nash's property, whether in slaves or money.) The Nash children sold Grandmother's fifth child, Benjamin, for $720, to Mr. Crawford. Ben was only ten years old. From then on, Grandmother worked even harder, hoping to eventually buy her five children from their owners.

One day, Mrs. Nash asked Grandmother to lend her $300 so that she could buy silver candlesticks. This was all the money that Grandmother had saved. Mrs. Nash promised to pay Grandmother back soon. No promise or written contract with a slave is legally binding, but Grandmother lent Mrs. Nash the money, believing that she would keep her promise.

When I was six, my mother died, and I learned, from the talk around me, that I was a slave. Everyone said that my mother had been a noble woman. I grieved for her. I was told that now I would live with Ruth Nash, my mother's white half-sister, and be her servant. When my mother was dying, Ruth Nash had promised her that she would take care of Willie and me and that we never would suffer or lack anything that we needed.

While I lived with Miss Nash, no one made me do difficult or unpleasant work. Miss Nash taught me to read and spell—a privilege given to very few slaves. She was so kind to me that I always was glad to do whatever she asked. I'd sit by her side for hours, doing her sewing and feeling as carefree as any freeborn white child. When Miss Nash thought that the sewing was making me tired, she'd send me out to play. I'd run and jump and gather flowers to decorate her room. Those were happy days.

When I was eleven, Miss Nash became ill. Her skin paled, and her eyes became glassy. I prayed with all my heart that she would live. She had been almost like a mother to me. But she died. Day after day I wept at her grave.

I wondered what the Nashes would do with Willie and me. My mother and I had loved Miss Nash and served her faithfully. I hoped that Miss Nash had arranged for me to be set free upon her death. But in her will she left me to her niece, Emily Flint, who was only five years old. Emily's young brother Nicholas would be Willie's new master.

Emily's father was Dr. Thomas Flint, a gray-haired, gray-eyed man who owned a fine Edenton residence, several plantations, and about fifty slaves. His wife Cora was much younger than he was. Willie and I would belong to Dr. and Mrs. Flint until Emily and Nicholas were old enough to have their own property. When people learned that Willie and I would be living with the Flints, there was much murmuring.

When Willie and I arrived at the Flints' Edenton house, we were greeted with cold looks, cold words, and cold treatment. That night, as I lay in my narrow bed, I wept.

It was even harder for Willie. He was free-spirited and hated having a master or mistress. One day, when Willie had been seven, Mrs. Jacobs and Father had called him at the same time. Willie had gone to Mrs. Jacobs. Father had scolded him, "You are *my* child. When I call you, you should come immediately, even if you have to walk through fire."

Like many Southern women, Mrs. Flint thought herself too weak to do any housework. But her nerves were strong enough for her to sit in her easy chair and watch a woman be whipped until she bled. Mrs. Flint went to church on Sundays. Afterward, if dinner wasn't served on time, she would wait until all the food had been served to her family and then spit into every bowl and pan that had been used. That way the cook couldn't feed left-overs to her own children.

At the Flints' house, slaves were allowed to eat only what Mrs. Flint chose to give them. Three times a day, she handed out small portions of cheap food. Fortunately, Grand-mother regularly gave me additional food that she had prepared.

If Dr. Flint was displeased with a particular dish, he would order either that the cook eat the entire dinner in his presence or that she be whipped. While the cook was breast-feeding her baby, Dr. and Mrs. Flint sometimes ordered her to leave the infant. Then they'd lock up the cook an entire day and night, leaving her baby with nothing to eat.

Once, the cook was ordered to make some cornmeal mush for the Flints' pet dog. The dog was too sick to eat. The Flints held his head over the food. Froth flowed from his mouth into the food. A few minutes later, he died. Dr. Flint said that the mush hadn't been cooked properly. He forced the cook to eat it. She became very ill.

One day, Dr. Flint had one of his plantation slaves, John, brought to Edenton. He ordered that John be tied up, in a shed, so that his feet were just above the ground. John hung this way while Flint had tea. Then Flint whipped John—hundreds of heavy blows. John kept begging, "Oh, pray don't, Master." The next morning I went into the shed. The walls and floor were covered with blood and gore. For months after, my ears rang with John's groans and pleas.

Why had John been whipped? John and his wife Daisy were black, but their newborn baby was very fair-skinned, so John had accused Dr. Flint of raping Daisy. (It's a crime for a slave woman to reveal the identity of a white man who has fathered her child.) Flint sold John and Daisy to a slave trader. That way, no one in Edenton would learn that he was the baby's father.

When Daisy was handed over to the trader, she cried out to Flint, "You promised to treat me well!"

Flint answered, "You talk too much. Damn you!"

Another young slave woman, Hannah, delivered a baby who was nearly white. The baby died, and Hannah herself was near death. She cried, "Oh Lord, come and take me, too!"

Sobbing, Hannah's mother said, "The baby is dead, thank God. I hope that my poor child will soon be in Heaven, too." She believed that life as a slave was worse than death.

Hannah's mistress said, "Heaven? Heaven is no place for her and her bastard baby. She deserves to suffer all this and more. You *all* do!"

As Hannah lay dying, she whispered to her mother, "Don't grieve, Mother. God knows what happened. *He* will have mercy on me."

# CHAPTER 2

After I'd been at the Flints' house for nearly a year, my friend Susie died. Her mother sobbed as clods of dirt fell onto Susie's coffin. Susie had been her only child. I turned away, thankful that I still had people to love.

Grandmother said, "Come with me, Harriet." When we were alone, she said, "My dear child, your father is dead."

I hadn't even heard that my father was sick. My heart rebelled against God. How could He have taken so many people away from me: my mother, my father, Miss Nash, and Susie?

Grandmother tried to comfort me. "Who knows God's ways? Perhaps He took them out of kindness, so that they wouldn't suffer through bad days to come."

The next day, I thought that the Flints at least would allow me to go to my father's home. But Mrs. Flint was having a party that evening. So, while my father's body lay less than a mile away, I was ordered to spend the day gathering flowers and decorating the Flints' house.

I tried to comfort Willie. "Take courage. Brighter days will come."

"No they won't," he said. "We'll have to stay here forever. We'll never be free."

"We're growing older and stronger. Soon we might be allowed to earn some money of our own. Before long we might have enough money to buy our freedom."

"I don't think so. Besides, we shouldn't *have* to buy our freedom. No one has the right to own anyone else."

When Grandmother was fifty, her mistress, Mrs. Nash, died. Dr. Flint was responsible for managing Mrs. Nash's will and property, so Grandmother asked him to return the $300 that she had lent to Mrs. Nash. Dr. Flint said that Mrs. Nash had been bankrupt when she died, so it would be illegal to pay Grandmother. He kept the silver candlesticks that Mrs. Nash had bought with Grandmother's money. I suppose that they'll remain in the Flint family and be handed down from generation to generation. Dr. Flint told Grandmother that he needed to sell her to help pay Mrs. Nash's debts.

Everyone in Edenton knew that Mrs. Nash's will said that Grandmother was to be set free. On the day of the auction, when Grandmother stepped up to be sold, many people called out, "Shame! Shame! You shouldn't be standing there, Aunt Martha. You're supposed to be free."

Grandmother stood there in silence. No one bid on her.

Finally, someone said, "Fifty dollars." It was Miss Fanny, Mrs. Nash's seventy-year-old sister.

The auctioneer waited for someone to offer a higher bid. No one did. Fanny paid Dr. Flint $50 and gave Grandmother her freedom. Everyone respected Fanny for her fairness and kindness.

Willie and I still belonged to the Flints.

At Dr. Flint's plantations, as on most Southern farms, slaves worked every spring day until all the corn and cotton had been planted. Then they had two days off. After that, they worked until Christmas Eve. If the slaves didn't break any rules, they often got four or five more days off.

On New Year's Eve, slaves gather their few possessions and wait anxiously for the next day. In the South, January 1st is the day when slaves are hired out or sold to other masters. At dawn all the slaves gather in the trading area and wait to hear their fate. They beg relatively kind masters, "Please, Master, hire me this year. I'll work very hard."

Any slaves who are hired by a cruel master and refuse to go are whipped and jailed until they agree to go and promise not to run away. If slaves are caught running away, they're whipped until the blood flows at their feet. Then their arms and legs are put into heavy chains, which they drag through the fields for days.

On New Year's Day a slave mother is terrified that her children will be taken from her. A slave trader may sell them, one by one, to whoever offers the highest price. Their mother wonders if they'd be better off dead.

I once encountered a slave woman after a trader had led away all seven of her children. She cried to me, "Gone! All gone! Why doesn't God kill me?"

# CHAPTER 3

One day when Willie was twelve and we'd spent two years with the Flints, he said, "Harriet, isn't this a bad world? I wish I had died when Father did."

I said, "As slave children and orphans, we can't expect to be happy, but we might find some satisfaction in being good."

"I try to be good, but what's the use? Nicholas is cowardly and cruel. He whips smaller boys but runs away when white boys his own size want to fight him. He said, 'I'm going to whip you' and tried to tie my hands behind me. I fought him off. He has no right to whip me!"

I said, "Be good and forgiving," but I loved Willie's defiant spirit.

One winter, Grandmother bought me a new pair of shoes to protect my feet from the snow. When Mrs. Flint called me to her room, the shoes creaked. "What a horrid noise!" she complained. "Take off those shoes. If you put them on again, I'll throw them into the fire."

Mrs. Flint then sent me on a long errand. I had to walk barefoot through several inches of snow. My feet tingled and became numb. My voice became hoarse. That night I went to bed thinking that I might be dead by morning. I was sorry to wake up alive and healthy.

Mrs. Flint hated me. She called me "the little devil." But Dr. Flint refused to sell me. Occasionally people offered him high prices for me. He always answered, "She doesn't belong to me. She's my daughter's property." Emily Flint was still a young child—too young to protect me. I loved her, and she seemed to love *me*. Mrs. Flint was jealous of Emily's affection for me.

Grandmother told me, "Pray to be satisfied with what you have."

Like Willie and my Uncle Ben, I couldn't accept enslavement. Not much older than I, Ben was smart and loving. One day when Crawford sent for him, Ben went only after some delay. Angry, Crawford began to whip him. Ben fought back and threw Crawford to the ground. Then he trembled in terror: he had raised his arm against his master, one of Edenton's richest men. For this, he would be publicly whipped.

That night, Ben sneaked out to see me. He said, "I've come to tell you goodbye, Harriet. I'm going north." His mouth was set with determination.

"Oh no, don't go!"

"I'm no longer a boy. Every day that I wear the chains of slavery, they feel heavier."

"You might be caught and brought back. You'd face terrible punishment. Or you'll face poverty and hardship in the North. You'll be alone among strangers."

"Isn't it better to face poverty and hardship as a free man than to be a slave? Harriet, here in the South we're treated like cattle or dogs. I won't stay. Let them bring me back. I can die only once."

I knew that Ben was right, but he was one of the few bright spots in my life; it was hard to give him up. I tried to make him feel guilty. "Go, then, and break your mother's heart." As soon as the words were out, I regretted having said them.

"Harriet, how can you say that? Poor Mother! Be good to her."

We exchanged heartfelt farewells.

Ben boarded a ship headed to New York. The captain saw a notice describing Ben and offering a reward for his return, so Ben was grabbed and chained. Before the ship reached New York, Ben managed to get free of the chains. He threw them overboard and escaped from the ship.

Ben was tracked down, captured, and

brought back to Crawford. He was led through Edenton's streets, in chains, to jail. His face was deathly pale but full of determination.

Grandmother and I weren't supposed to visit Ben. But the jailer was a kind man who had known us for years. He opened the jail door at midnight so that Grandmother and I, in disguise, could see Ben.

Ben said, "Mother, please forgive me for having caused you to suffer."

"There's nothing to forgive," Grandmother said. "I can't blame you for wanting freedom."

"When I broke out of my chains, I considered throwing myself into the ocean. Thinking of you prevented me from doing that."

"Did you also think of God?"

Ben's face turned fierce. "No. When a man is hunted like a wild beast, he forgets that there's a God. He forgets *everything* in his struggle to get beyond the bloodhounds' reach."

"Don't talk that way, Ben. Put your trust in God. Be humble, my child, and Crawford will forgive you."

"Forgive me for *what*, Mother? For not letting him treat me like a dog? No! I never will humble myself to him. All my life I've worked for him without pay. Now I'm repaid by being whipped and jailed. I'll stay here until he sells me or I die."

Grandmother shuddered.

Ben continued more calmly. "Don't worry about me, Mother. I'm not worth it. I wish I had some of your goodness. You accept everything so patiently. I wish that *I* could."

After Ben had been in prison for three weeks, Grandmother pleaded with Crawford to release him. Crawford wanted Ben to serve as an example to the rest of his slaves. He said that he'd keep Ben in jail until Ben asked for forgiveness or someone offered to buy him.

Three months passed. One day someone heard Ben singing and laughing and reported this to Crawford. After that, Ben was confined in a cell with other prisoners, who were clothed in filthy rags. Soon Ben was covered with lice. Ben worked at his chains until he removed them. Then he passed them through the bars of his cell. "Please have someone take these to Crawford," he told the jailer, "with the message that I'm covered with lice."

As punishment for his boldness, Ben was bound with heavier chains. Grandmother and I no longer were allowed to visit him.

Three months later, Crawford sold Ben to a slave trader. Because Ben was known to have rebelled, and because confinement had made him weak and thin, he was worth less at age twenty than he had been at age ten. Crawford had bought him for $720, but the slave trader paid only $300. The trader said that it would have been different if the handsome, light-skinned fellow had been a woman; in that case, he would have paid any price. Grandmother and I thanked God that Ben was a man.

Grandmother clung to Ben as they chained him. She looked from face to face, begging for mercy—in vain. She asked the trader if she could buy Ben.

The trader said, "Not within the state. I agreed not to sell him within North Carolina. But I'll promise you not to sell him before we reach New Orleans."

Grandmother labored day and night in the hope of buying Ben. The trader wanted $900—triple the price that he had paid.

Ben escaped on a ship bound for Baltimore. Because of his white face, no one suspected that he was a slave.

While Ben was in Baltimore, anxious to continue north, someone called out, "Hello, Ben, my boy! What are you doing here?" There stood Crawford's next-door neighbor! "Why, you look like a ghost. I guess I gave you a shock. Never mind. I won't harm you. I know you've had a tough time. I advise you to get out of Baltimore right away. Several Edenton gentlemen are here. They might see you." He told Ben the fastest, safest route to New York. "I'll be glad to tell your mother that I've seen you. Goodbye, Ben."

Although this man had married a Southerner, he was a Northerner by birth. He hadn't forgotten that slaves are human beings. Ben was surprised that such a good man lived in Edenton.

Ben reached New York safely. His brother, my Uncle Phillip, had been sent to New York on business for his mistress. The brothers met.

Ben said, "Phil, when I was in jail, I didn't think that life was worth living, but now I'm free. Stay, and work with me. Together we'll earn enough money to buy the rest of the family."

"Ben, it would kill Mother if I deserted her. She has raised enough money to buy you. Will you let her do that?"

"Never! I'll never give Crawford a penny. How could I let Mother spend all her hard-earned money to buy me, when she won't ever see me again? You know that she won't leave the South as long as any of her other children are slaves. Tell her to buy *you*, Phil. You've been a comfort to her. I've been only trouble. And what about poor Harriet? What will become of *her*? I wish Dr. Flint were dead. I hate him more than I hate Crawford."

When the brothers parted, their eyes were wet with tears. As Ben turned away, he said sadly, "Phil, I must leave behind my entire family."

And so it was. We never heard from Ben again.

As soon as Uncle Phillip came home, he told Grandmother the wonderful news. "Ben is free! I've seen him in New York."

Grandmother raised her hands and exclaimed, "God be praised! Let us thank Him!"

Grandmother kept up her work, hoping to buy some of her other children. After a while she succeeded in buying Phillip. She paid $800 for him and came home with the bill of sale, the precious document that secured his freedom. That night the happy mother and son sat together, saying how proud they were of each other.

# CHAPTER 4

When I was fifteen, Dr. Flint, who was fifty-five, began to whisper obscenities in my ear. No law protects a slave woman from insult, violence, or even death. An attractive white woman is admired, but an attractive black woman is humiliated and brutalized.

Sometimes Flint cursed and threatened me; sometimes he tried to seduce me with gentleness. He told me that I was his property and must surrender to his will. I tried to ignore him, but I was forced to live in his house. He met me at every turn. If I went out for some fresh air after a day of hard work, he followed me. If I knelt at my mother's grave, his shadow fell across me. The other slaves in the Flints' house noticed that I looked anxious and depressed, and they knew why. They also knew that they'd be punished if they talked about Flint's lechery.

Flint said that he'd kill me if I told anyone. I feared that if Grandmother found out, she'd endanger both of us: once, she had chased a white man with a loaded pistol after he insulted one of her daughters.

One day Flint caught me teaching myself to write. At first he was displeased. Then he took advantage of my ability to read by handing me obscene notes.

Sometimes Flint ate dinner alone on the porch. He'd order me to stand close to him and brush away the flies. He'd eat very slowly. Between mouthfuls he'd tell me that I was throwing away my chance at happiness by not submitting to him. "I'd cherish you. I'd make a lady of you."

When I would manage to avoid him around the house, he'd order me to come to his office, where he'd make disgusting comments. If I responded disdainfully, he'd become enraged. But he wouldn't hit me.

Sometimes he'd ask me if I wanted to be sold. I'd tell him that anything would be better than the life that I was leading. Then he'd act as if his feelings were hurt. "Didn't I take you into my house? I've never let anyone touch you, not even when your mistress wanted you to be punished."

He knew that if he whipped me, people might talk about him and reveal his dirty secret to his children, grandchildren, and patients. Flint was the father of eleven slave children. Mrs. Flint had known, for years, about her husband's indecent behavior toward his female slaves. Instead of trying to protect these women, she treated them with meanness and suspicion.

Flint announced that he was going to have his four-year-old daughter sleep in his bedroom. In case the child woke up during the night, he wanted a servant to sleep in the same room. He chose me. I refused. In an effort to force me to comply, he held a razor to my throat.

Fortunately, my mother's twin sister, Aunt Nancy, also lived in the Flints' house. Aunt Nancy was the housekeeper and Mrs. Flint's personal servant. I started sleeping beside Aunt Nancy because Dr. Flint never would dare to enter her room.

The first night, Dr. Flint stayed alone with his little girl. Then he ordered me to stay in his room the following night. Mrs. Flint heard about the plan and raged at him. Then she called me to her room. She made me put my hand on a Bible and swear before God that I'd tell her the truth. She said, "Sit on this stool, look me in the face, and tell me everything that has gone on between your master and you."

I described what Dr. Flint had done. As Mrs. Flint listened, she groaned and wept, but only for herself.

Dr. Flint had to abandon his plan. Mrs. Flint had me sleep in the room next to hers. She continued to worry about whether I had submitted to her husband's demands. Hoping to hear me talk in my sleep, she would bend over me while I slept. It was frightening to wake up in the middle of the night and find an angry, jealous woman bending over me.

In an effort to trick her husband into revealing something, Mrs. Flint said to him, in front of me, "She says that you've raped her."

Dr. Flint responded, "You must have tortured her into making such an unbelievable accusation."

Some Northerners are proud if their daughter marries a Southern slave owner. But the young wife soon learns that her husband readily breaks his marriage vows. Slave women who are servants in her house give birth to children with lighter skin. The wife then realizes that these must be her husband's children. She watches these children play with her own babies. Jealousy and hatred darken her home.

Many Southern women will marry a man even though they know that he has fathered many slaves. As soon as possible, these women get their husband's slave children out of sight by selling them.

However, I knew two Southern wives who successfully begged their husbands to free their slave children. Also, some Southern ladies consider it disgraceful for slave owners to father slaves. "I declare," I heard one Southern lady say, "such things should not be tolerated in any decent society."

While Dr. Flint continued to harass me, I fell in love with Ned, a young carpenter who was intelligent and pious. Ned was black, but he'd been born free. He wanted to buy me so that I could legally become his wife.

Like many other mistresses, Mrs. Flint thought that slaves had no right to family ties of their own. In her view, slaves should devote themselves to their *master's* family. Once, I heard Mrs. Flint threaten a young slave woman named Eve, who asked permission to marry a black man named Joe. Eve already had one child, who was light-skinned. (Dr. Flint, of course, didn't admit that he was the father.) Joe would have gladly accepted this child as his own. Mrs. Flint yelled at Eve, "Don't ever mention that subject again! I won't have you care for my children alongside the children of that nigger!"

One day I asked a kind white lady, a friend of Dr. Flint, if she would try to persuade him to let Ned buy me. She tried but failed.

The next morning, Dr. Flint ordered me

into his study. When I entered, he glared at me. "So you want to be married, do you? And to a free nigger!"

"Yes, Sir."

"*I'm* your master, not the nigger fellow you honor so highly. If you *must* have a husband, you may live with one of my slaves."

"Don't you think, Sir, that a slave has some preferences about whom she marries? Do you think that all men are alike to her?"

"Do you love this nigger?"

"Yes."

"I thought you felt above the insults proposed by such black puppies."

"If he's a puppy, then I'm a puppy too. We're both black. It's right and honorable for us to love each other. Ned never has insulted me."

Flint sprang at me and struck me hard. It was the first time that he ever had hit me.

I was stunned. When I recovered, I said, "You hit me because I answered you honestly. I despise you!"

After some minutes of silence, he said, "I have a right to do whatever I want with you."

"You do *not* have that right."

"How dare you speak to me so disrespectfully! Many masters would kill you on the spot. How would you like to go to jail?"

"I'd have more peace in jail than I do *here*."

"I'll give you one more chance. If you behave and do what I say, I'll forgive you and treat you as I always have. But if you disobey me, I'll punish you as harshly as I'd punish the most worthless plantation slave. Never mention that fellow's name to me again. If I ever find out that you've been speaking to him, I'll whip you both. If I catch him on my property, I'll shoot him."

For two weeks Dr. Flint didn't speak to me, but he watched me closely. Then I encountered Ned on the street in front of Flint's house and stopped to speak to him. Looking up, I saw Flint watching us from his window. I hurried back inside, trembling with fear. I immediately was ordered to Flint's study.

As soon as I entered, Flint hit me. "When is Mistress Harriet going to be married?" he sneered. I was so thankful that Ned was free! Flint didn't have the right to beat a free man.

Even if Ned and I married, Ned wouldn't be able to protect me from Flint, who still would be my master. Some slave men fight to protect their wife and daughters from their master's abuse and boldly protest to their master. But many—whipped into submission—voice no objection. In fact, some purposely stay away when the master wants sex with their wife or daughter.

Any children born to Ned and me would be Dr. Flint's property because children have the same legal status—enslaved or free—as their mother.

For *his* sake, I begged Ned to go to the Free States and never return. In the North he'd be able to speak freely and make full use of his intelligence. Hoping that someday he'd be able to buy me, Ned left. I felt empty and alone.

Willie and I talked about trying to escape. But we had no money, and I was closely watched. Also, Grandmother didn't want us to run away. She feared that we'd be captured and severely punished, like Ben.

Slave owners lie to slaves about what happens to those who escape to the North. One slave owner told me that he'd seen a runaway friend of mine in New York. He said that she was starving: many days she had only one cold potato to eat; other days she had nothing. He said that she'd begged him to take her back to her master but he'd refused, saying that her master wouldn't want such a miserable wretch. "This is the punishment she brought on herself for running away from a kind master." My friend later would tell me that the whole story was false.

But many slaves believe such stories. They think it isn't worth trading slavery for such harsh freedom. Most slaves can't read, so they believe what their masters tell them.

Slave owners seem to satisfy their consciences by saying that God created blacks to be their slaves. Are blacks really any different from whites? And how much white blood runs in the veins of American slaves?

A master may be highly educated, dress like a gentleman, and consider himself a Christian, but if an enslaved man resists whipping, the master might command his bloodhounds to tear the man's flesh from his bones. If a runaway woman is captured and brought back, her master might shoot her through the head.

Mr. Litch, who was uneducated and crude, owned a nearby plantation and six hundred slaves. He required strict obedience to the commandment "Thou shall not steal." Of course, *he* stole labor from his slaves. But if his hungry slaves stole any food from *him*, he chained and imprisoned them until they were thin from starvation. One of his favorite punishments was to tie up a naked man and roast a piece of fatty pork over him. As the pork cooked, scalding drops of fat would fall onto the man's bare flesh. Litch was so wealthy that no one questioned any of his crimes, including murder.

One stormy winter evening when he was half drunk, another slave owner became annoyed with one of his servants. He stripped the slave of all but his shirt, whipped him, tied him to a tree, and left him there for three hours. The wind blew bitterly cold. The tree's branches crackled under falling sleet. When the slave was cut loose, he was more dead than alive.

Some slave owners try to be "humane," but they are few and far between. Miss Nelson inherited a slave woman named Bess and her children. Miss Nelson freed Bess's oldest daughter the day before she was to marry a free man, so that the marriage would be legally binding. Later Mr. Hampton, a young man who was attracted to her money, proposed to Miss Nelson. Before marrying him, Miss Nelson offered Bess and her children freedom: "Once I'm married, I won't have the same power; I want to make sure that you're happy." Bess declined the offer, saying that she and her children never could be as happy anywhere else as they were with Miss Nelson. Hampton proved to be a cruel master. Bess's husband, a free man named Michael, hid the children in the woods. They soon were found. Hampton jailed Michael and sold the two oldest boys to a slave owner in Georgia. He brought the oldest enslaved daughter, Jane, to his plantation and fathered two children by her. Then he sold Jane and her two children to his brother. Jane had two children by Hampton's brother and was sold again.

Slavery corrupts the owners. The master's sons are corrupted by their father's immoral behavior. The master's daughters hear their parents fighting about slave women and may overhear talk of their father having seduced or raped slaves. Sometimes a young white woman uses the same power over male slaves that her father uses over female slaves. An infant born to a white woman and a slave may be sent where no one knows the baby's history or may be smothered. But there's no shame when the father is a white master and the mother is a black slave. If the child is female, when she is fourteen or fifteen, her owner, his sons, the overseer, or all of them bribe her for sex. If she refuses to submit, they whip or starve her. Slavery makes the white fathers cruel and obscene, their sons violent and immoral, their daughters impure, and their wives miserable. But slave owners don't worry about their children's ruined character; they worry only about ruined crops.

# CHAPTER 5

Many Edenton residents gossiped about how Dr. Flint was harassing me. Mrs. Flint added to the gossip by openly talking about her husband's behavior. Grandmother heard about Dr. Flint and told him what she thought of him.

Mr. Sands, an educated, unmarried white man who knew Grandmother, kindly asked me about Dr. Flint's treatment of me, and I told him some of the things that Flint had done. Sands said that he'd like to help me. He often visited me and wrote to me. Only fifteen, I was flattered by his attention and grateful for his sympathy and generosity. Gradually I developed more tender feelings toward him. Also, I liked the idea of getting revenge on Flint. I thought that if Sands and I became lovers, Flint would sell me when he found out about the relationship; then Sands would buy me and set me free. I also thought that Sands would secure the freedom of any children born to us. I became his lover.

31

Some months later, Flint told me that he had built a small house for me, in an isolated place four miles from Edenton. He ordered me to go to this house.

I refused.

"You will go, even if you have to be carried there."

"I never will go there. In a few months I'll be a mother."

Shocked, he stared at me. He left the house without a word.

I had thought that I'd be happy in my triumph over him, but I was miserable. Now my relatives would learn of my relationship with Sands. They had been so proud of my good character. How could I look them in the eye? My self-respect was gone.

I went to tell Grandmother. Before I could get the words out, Mrs. Flint came in—crazed—and accused me of being pregnant with her husband's child.

Grandmother believed her. "Oh, Harriet! Has it come to this? I'd rather see you dead. You're a disgrace to your dead mother." She tore my mother's wedding ring from my finger. "Go away! Never come to my house again!"

Sobbing too much to speak, I left Grandmother's house. I walked for miles, not caring where I went or what became of me. I prayed to die.

Finally I returned to Grandmother and kneeled in front of her. I told her about Sands, described how Dr. Flint had harassed me, and said that I'd been desperate to escape Flint's abuse. I begged her to forgive me.

She did not say, "I forgive you," but she looked at me lovingly, her eyes full of tears. She gently touched my head and murmured, "Poor child!"

Mrs. Flint wouldn't allow me to return to her house, so I stayed with Grandmother. Grandmother met with Sands, who promised to care for my child and to buy me, whatever the cost.

After five days, Dr. Flint came to see me. He said that I had disgraced myself, shamed my grandmother, and sinned against *him*. He hinted that he could perform an abortion. Then no one else would know that I had sinned. He asked, "Is the father of your child the fellow you wanted to marry? Don't lie to me. If you do, you'll feel the fires of hell."

I didn't answer.

"Damn you! I'll leave now, but I'll be back tomorrow."

Flint returned the next day, looking unhappy. He ordered me to stand up in front of him. I obeyed. "I command you to tell me whether the father of your child is white or black," he said.

I hesitated.

"Answer me this instant!"

"He's white."

Flint jumped at me and grabbed my arm as if he wanted to break it. "Do you love him?"

"I'm thankful that *he* isn't someone I hate."

Flint raised his hand to hit me, but he stopped and stepped away. "I'll take care of you and your child, but only if you have nothing further to do with the father. You must not communicate with him or receive anything from him. You'd better agree to this now and not wait until he has deserted you."

"I'm not willing to have my child supported by a man who has cursed both my child and me."

"A woman who has sunk to your level has no right to expect anything else. For the last time, will you accept my kindness?"

"No."

"Very well. Never look to me for help. You're my slave, and you'll always be my slave. I'll never sell you." He left.

At this time Flint was using Willie in his office. Willie had taught himself to read and write; he was intelligent and useful. Flint took his anger out on Willie. One morning Willie didn't arrive at the office quite as early as usual, and Flint used this as an excuse to jail him.

The next day Willie boldly sent a slave trader to ask Flint to sell him. Flint said that Willie was being disrespectful. He was angry that Willie refused to apologize to him. But Flint couldn't find anyone else who could do Willie's work; without Willie everything went wrong at the office. So after two days, Flint released Willie from jail and ordered him back to work.

I became so ill in mind and body that I couldn't get out of bed. I refused to see Flint, and he wouldn't let me see any other doctor. I prayed that I would die. Finally my family and friends were so worried about me that they asked Flint to come. As soon as he entered my room, I started to scream. He left.

My baby was born prematurely; he weighed only four pounds. I named him Benny, after my Uncle Ben. I no longer wanted to die, not unless Benny also died.

I was bedridden for many weeks. Benny, too, was very ill. He suffered terrible pain in his little arms and legs. Dr. Flint came often. He repeatedly reminded me that Benny belonged to *him*.

As the months passed, Benny's health slowly improved. When Benny was a year old, everyone said that he was beautiful. His clinging attachment to me made me feel both love and pain. I never could forget that he was a slave.

# CHAPTER 6

Everyone in Edenton heard about a rebellion against slavery, led by Nat Turner. Several whites in Virginia had been killed. Most whites in Edenton were terrified that the slave rebellion might spread to North Carolina. Turner hadn't been captured yet, so whites wanted to find out which blacks supported him and which had weapons.

On the day of a military parade, whites poured into Edenton from the surrounding countryside. Country gentlemen and Edenton's well-to-do men wore military uniforms. Poor white men wore everyday clothes. They all marched to military music.

Suddenly orders were given and all the men rushed in every direction, wherever they could find a black. It was a grand opportunity for poor whites, who had no slaves of their own to whip, to bully other people's slaves. Poor whites regularly showed their loyalty to wealthy slave owners. They never stopped to think about what they had in common with slaves. The same power that slave owners used to trample blacks kept these whites poor, ignorant, and immoral.

The white men started searching black homes, looking for signs that the occupants were involved in rebellion. Sometimes a group of searchers put their own gunshot among black people's clothes. Then they sent another group of searchers to the house, where they found this "proof" that the blacks were planning to shoot whites. Everywhere, black men, women, and children were whipped until their blood formed puddles at their feet. Some were given five hundred lashes. Others had their hands and feet tied and were rubbed with a rough paddle until they were covered with blisters. The searchers robbed blacks of clothing and anything else that they thought was worth carrying away.

All day white men terrified and tormented blacks. At night some of them raped black women. If a black husband or father reported the crime, he was tied to the public whipping post and whipped for "lying." People with even the slightest brownness to their skin were afraid to be seen talking together.

*I* wasn't afraid because my family was surrounded by whites who would protect us. I knew that the white bullies hated to see blacks leading comfortable, respectable lives. To annoy them, I made Grandmother's house look as tidy and pretty as possible. I put white quilts on the beds and flowers in some of the rooms.

Before long we heard voices and the tramp of feet. Searchers pushed the door open and rushed in. They snatched at everything within their reach. They examined every closet, trunk, and box. In one drawer they found a box with some silver coins in it. They pounced on this. I stepped forward to take the box from them.

A poor white angrily said, "Why are you watching us? Do you think we've come to steal?"

I answered, "You've come to search. Now that you've searched that box, I'll take it back, please."

Just then I looked out the window and saw a white man who was friendly to us. I asked him if he would come inside and stay until the search ended. He did.

One of the searchers shouted with surprise. He'd found a trunk filled with linens. "Where did these damned niggers get all these sheets and tablecloths?"

Knowing that our white friend would protect her, Grandmother said, "We certainly didn't steal them from *your* house "

Another man said, "Look here, Mammy. You seem to feel mighty important just because you've got all this fancy stuff. White folks should have all of it."

Some of the men started shouting, "We've got the niggers now! This yellow gal's got *letters*!"

Because none of these men could read, they sent for their captain. He was Litch, the cruel slave owner. Litch told his men that the "letters" were just some poems that a friend had written to me. His men were disappointed.

Litch demanded, "Who wrote these poems?"

I said, "A friend of mine."

"Can you read them?"

"Yes."

Swearing and ranting, he tore one of the poems to pieces. "Bring me all your letters!"

"I don't have any others."

Changing his tone, he said, "Don't be afraid. Nobody will hurt you. Bring them all to me."

I didn't move.

He started threatening me. "Who writes to you? Free niggers?"

"No. Most of my letters have been from whites."

A shout of surprise came from another room. The men had discovered Grandmother's silver spoons. Then they found a closet full of fruit preserves that Grandmother had made for customers. They opened a jar and started helping themselves.

I stretched out my hand to take back the jar. "You weren't sent here to search for preserves."

"So show me what we *are* looking for," Litch said.

I didn't respond.

Litch's men finished searching the house and left with some of our clothing. Litch cursed the house, saying that it should be burned to the ground and that each person in it should get thirty-nine lashes.

By evening the searchers were drunk. A mob dragged some blacks down the street. One prisoner was an elderly minister. The searchers had found a few small bundles of gunshot that his wife used as weights on food-measuring scales. Because of this, they were going to shoot the minister in the town square. Some of Edenton's upper-class whites saved him.

At last Edenton's white citizens realized that the drunken mob was endangering *their* property, so they sent the searchers back into the countryside. However, for two weeks Edenton whites continued to persecute blacks.

One form of persecution was to tie a black man to a horse's saddle forcing him to run alongside, and then ride the horse while whipping the man, who would pant in an effort to keep pace with the horse's speed. In some cases, the black man was whipped so much that he no longer could walk. When he collapsed, he was washed with saltwater, thrown into a cart, and brought to jail.

Threatened with whipping, one black man made up a story about the rebellion. In reality, he knew nothing about it. He never even had heard of Nat Turner. The story he made up caused him, and other blacks, to suffer even more.

Nothing was proved against any of the persecuted blacks, free or enslaved. Finally Turner was captured and executed. At last the prisoners were released. Slaves were sent back to their masters. Free blacks returned to looted, wrecked homes.

But Edenton's blacks still were forbidden to congregate. They begged to be allowed to pray together in a little church that they had built in the woods. Whites destroyed the church. Blacks were allowed to go to white churches, where they had to sit in the balcony. White worshipers always received the sacramental bread and wine before the blacks.

Slave owners wanted to prevent another

slave rebellion, so they decided to teach their slaves just enough religion to keep them from murdering their masters. The Episcopal minister, Reverend Pike, offered to hold a separate service for slaves on Sunday evenings.

At the first service, Pike sermonized, "You are rebellious sinners. God is pleased when you serve your masters faithfully and angry when you do not. When you tell lies, God hears you. When you steal from your masters, God sees you. He will punish you. Obey your masters. If you disobey your earthly master, you offend God, your heavenly Master."

With some other slaves, I went to a study group at the Methodist church. Edenton's sheriff led the class. He was a slave trader and lashed his fellow churchgoers at the public whipping post. For fifty cents he was happy to perform a whipping anywhere.

This "Christian" came over to Paula, who was sitting next to me. Paula's last child just had been sold. The sheriff said, "Tell us, Sister. Do you love God as much as before?"

"My load is more than I can bear," Paula said. Her voice was so sorrowful that some of the other slaves started to cry. "They've got all my children now. Last week they took the last one. God only knows where they've sold her. They let me keep her for sixteen years. Then . . . Oh! Pray for my child and for her brothers and sisters. I've got nothing to live for now. God, make my time on earth short!"

The sheriff covered his mouth so that we wouldn't see him laughing. He had us sing a hymn: "The Devil's earthly church is here below. God's heavenly church is where I hope to go."

Reverend Pike soon left Edenton; he went to a church where he could make more money. Reverend Winston took his place. He brought five slaves with him. His wife taught them reading, writing, and other skills. Reverend Winston tried to help the needy slaves around him. We all said, "God has sent us a good man this time." Black children loved Reverend Winston; he always gave them a smile or a kind word.

Every Sunday evening, Reverend Winston led a special service for slaves. His sermons were simple, so everyone could understand them. Many blacks started going to his church every Sunday because they enjoyed his preaching. Many of them never before had known a white man who spoke to them as human beings.

"Try to live according to God's word, my friends," Reverend Winston would say. "Your skin is darker than mine, but God judges people by the goodness of their hearts, not by the color of their skin." This was a strange thing to preach in a Southern church. It offended many slave owners. The church's white members started complaining. They said that their slaves were being ruined by Reverend Winston and his wife.

If a Southern man gives money to his church, he is called religious. It doesn't matter if he has gotten the money by abusing slaves. If a religious leader has children by a white woman who isn't his wife, he must leave the church. But if he has children by a black slave, he is allowed to go on telling church members how to act like Christians.

Reverend Winston's wife became fatally ill. Her slaves gathered around her in sorrow. Just before she died, she told her slaves, "I leave you all free. May we meet again in a better world." Her former slaves left Edenton with money that Reverend Winston gave them to start new lives. Soon after that, Reverend Winston preached his last sermon to us. We shed many tears when he went away.

I knew a black man named Fred, who first joined the Baptist church when he was fifty-three. He believed that he could serve God better if he could read the Bible. Fred came to me and begged me to teach him to read. He had no money, but he offered to bring me fruit from his trees. I knew that it was against the law for one slave to teach another to read.

If a teacher and student were caught, both were whipped and jailed. I agreed to teach Fred in secret. As soon as he could spell, he wanted to spell out words in the Bible. After six months, he had read the entire New Testament. I asked him how he had learned so quickly.

He said, "Every time I come for a lesson, I pray to God to help me understand what I spell and read, and He *does* help me."

There are thousands of slaves like Fred who thirst for knowledge. Missionaries go all over the world to teach people about God, but they don't see the needs of people in their own country. They tell Africans that it's wrong to buy and sell people, but they don't tell American slave owners that it's wrong to own slaves and to violate slave women.

A few good men try to do missionary work among the slaves. The South hates them. When they're caught, they're chased away or dragged to prison.

After Reverend Winston left, Dr. Flint joined the Episcopal Church. I hoped that religion would improve his behavior, but he harassed me most on his way home from church. One Sunday he spoke to me so obscenely that I reminded him that he had just joined the church.

"Yes, Harriet. I decided to join the church

because my position in society requires it. Being a church member puts an end to all the damned slander. You would do well to join the church, too."

"There are enough sinners in it already," I said. "I'd be happy to go if I were allowed to *live* like a Christian."

"You can do what I request. If you're faithful to me, you'll be as virtuous as my wife."

"That's not what the Bible says."

"How dare you preach to me about your damned Bible!"

No wonder slaves sing, "The Devil's earthly church is here below. God's heavenly church is where I hope to go."

# CHAPTER 7

Sometimes Dr. Flint threatened to sell Benny. "Maybe that will humble you," he said. His threat ripped my heart. What would happen if Benny fell into a slave trader's hands?

Once, in a moment of passion, Flint threw me down the stairs. He hurt me so badly that I couldn't turn myself in bed for many days. He said, "Harriet, I swear to God that I'll never raise my hand against you again."

When Flint learned that I was going to have another child, he came to Grandmother's house with scissors. He often had accused me of being proud of my hair. Now, swearing at me, he cut my hair close to my head. Each time I said something, he hit me.

At the age of nineteen, I gave birth to a girl. My heart nearly broke. Slavery is terrible for men, but it is even worse for women.

Four days after my daughter was born, I still was too weak to stand up very long. Suddenly Flint entered my room and ordered me to get up and bring my baby over to him.

"Stand there until I tell you to sit down!"

Flint noticed that my daughter looked like her father, Mr. Sands. While I stood trembling with weakness, Flint cursed me and my baby. I fainted. He threw cold water into my face and shook me. Just then Grandmother came in. Flint hurried from the house.

One Sunday when Flint was out of town, Grandmother said, "This is our chance. We can have the children baptized."

When I walked into the church, I remembered how my mother had brought me to my own baptism. Unlike me, my mother had been married. I was glad that she wasn't alive to witness my shame.

Sands had said that the children could have his last name, but I decided to give them the last name of my father's former owners: Jacobs. Just before the church service, Mrs. Jacobs suggested that I also give my daughter her *first* name, Ellen.

After the service, Mrs. Jacobs placed a gold chain around Ellen's neck. I thanked her for her kind gift, but I didn't like what it symbolized. I didn't want any chains on Ellen, even if they were gold.

Benny and Ellen grew beautiful and strong. Dr. Flint often said with a triumphant smile, "One of these days these brats will make a lot of money for me." I prayed that they never would fall into his hands.

I had friends who wanted to buy my freedom. They asked a slave trader to offer Flint as much as $1,200. Flint told the trader, "She doesn't belong to me. She's my daughter's property. I suspect that her lover sent you. You may tell him that he can't buy her for any price. He can't buy her children, either." Flint loved money, but he loved power even more.

Flint came to see me the next day. My heart beat faster when he entered the house. Benny and Ellen also had learned to fear him. Whenever Ellen saw him, she shut her eyes and hid her face against my shoulder. Benny, who was almost five, often asked me, "What makes that bad man come here so much? Does he want to hurt us?"

Flint said, "Your lover is trying to buy you?" He grabbed my arm, dragged me out of my chair, and started cursing me.

Benny started to scream. I told him to go to Grandmother.

"Don't move a step, you wretch!" Flint yelled at Benny, who put his arms around me as if to protect me. This made Flint even angrier. He grabbed Benny and threw him across the room.

Terrified that Benny was dead, I rushed over to him. He was unconscious.

Flint yelled, "Let him lie there until he

comes to!"

Somebody opened the front door, and Flint left. I bent over Benny, who was pale and still. At last his brown eyes opened.

Out of jealousy, Flint came to see me morning, noon, and night. One day he searched Grandmother's house, expecting to find Sands there. Instead he found a young woman named Rose. Flint had abused Rose for years and just had sold her to a slave trader. She was staying in Grandmother's house until the trader was ready to leave town.

Flint ordered Rose to leave the house. Because he no longer was her master, she ignored him.

Flint turned to me. "What gives you the right to keep this girl here, when you know that I've sold her?"

"Rose came to see my grandmother. She is most welcome here."

Because Rose no longer was his slave, Flint couldn't hit her, so he took his anger out on *me*. Grandmother walked in just as he was hitting me. Flint told her that I'd been rude.

Grandmother yelled, "Get out of my house! Go home, and take care of your own wife and children, instead of watching *my* family."

Flint accused her of allowing me to lead a sinful life.

"You're to blame," she said. "You'd better start saying your prayers. When you die, you'll need all of them—and more—to wash the dirt off your soul."

Flint left the house in a rage. He returned some weeks later and said to me, "If you agree to my conditions, you and your children will be free. First, you must not communicate in any way with their father. Second, you must live in a cottage that I'll buy for you. I'll allow you to live there with your children. Your work will be light, such as sewing for my family. Think what I'm offering you: a home and freedom. Perhaps I've been harsh with you at times. That's because you've been stubborn and disobedient." Flint paused for an answer.

I remained silent.

"Why don't you speak? What more do you want?"

"Nothing, Sir."

"Then, you accept my offer?"

"No."

He barely controlled his anger. "Either you accept my offer, or you and your children will be sent to my son's plantation. There your children will be treated like the rest of the slave children. I'll give you one week to think about it."

I knew that he had no intention of freeing Benny, Ellen, and me. Once he had me in a cottage away from town, no one would see what he did or be able to protect me. I also thought that he wouldn't let me stay on his son's plantation very long. He would be too jealous of his son and the plantation overseer.

"I'm ready to give my answer now," I said.

"I won't accept it now." He left.

Flint returned a week later. "I hope you've made a wise choice."

I said, "I'm ready to go to the plantation, Sir."

"Very well. Go to the plantation. My curse goes with you. Your boy will be put to hard work. Soon he'll be sold. Your girl will be raised so that she can be sold for a large profit. Go your own ways!" He left the room, cursing.

"What did you tell him?" Grandmother asked.

"I told him that I'm going to the plantation."

"Do you have to go? Can't anything be done to stop it?"

"I don't think so."

Grandmother went to Flint and offered to pay him enough to buy another woman who would do what he wanted.

He refused. "I'm doing this for Harriet's own good. She's much too proud for a slave. She needs to learn humility and obedience.

Living on the plantation will teach her to behave."

The next morning, I left Grandmother's house to go to the plantation. I took Ellen with me but had to leave Benny behind because he was ill. I was determined to make my stay on the plantation as short as possible.

When Ellen and I arrived, Dr. Flint's son George sent Ellen to play by herself in the yard. She was used to having an adult look after her, but I wasn't allowed to see her until noon. By then, she had sobbed herself to sleep.

I was in charge of running the household. George Flint was going to marry in six weeks, and he wanted the house fixed up before his bride arrived. He often inspected the house to make sure that everyone was working hard.

One day I heard Mr. Flint tell his neighbor, "I've got her down here so that I can take those fancy town ideas out of her head. My father is partly to blame for her nonsense. He should have broken her in long ago."

Mr. Flint said many things to me that might have shocked his neighbor. He was no different from his father.

I worked day and night and tried to look happy. I saw how Mr. Flint beat the little slave children. I watched as their mothers stood by, too afraid to stop him. Whippings had crushed their spirit. I began to feel that I'd rather see Ellen die than see her beaten by Mr. Flint.

Ellen was kept separated from me, with no one to look after her. All day she wandered around by herself. One morning she cried such a weary cry that my heart bled. After a while, her crying stopped. I looked out the window. She was gone. I looked for her and found her under the house, which was raised two feet above the ground. She was fast asleep. I crept under the house and carried her out. I sat on the ground, holding her in my arms. I said to her sadly, "I sometimes think it would be better if you never woke up."

"Were you speaking to *me*?" Mr. Flint was standing right beside me. He said nothing else. Frowning, he turned away. That night, to my surprise, Mr. Flint sent Ellen a biscuit and a cup of sweetened milk.

The next day, I sent Ellen to Grandmother's house. Mr. Flint said that I should have asked his permission first. I said, "Ellen was sick, and I had too much work to care for her."

After three weeks on the plantation, I sneaked home to see Ellen, Benny, and Grandmother. I waited until late at night, after everybody was in bed and then went with Matthew, a young man who often sneaked into Edenton to see his mother. It was six miles to Edenton, but fear made us walk quickly.

When I arrived at the house, Grandmother smiled and cried.

I looked in on Benny and Ellen, who were sleeping. As I turned to leave, Benny moved. I whispered to him, "Mother is here."

After rubbing his eyes with his little fists, Benny opened them wide and said, "Oh, Mother! You aren't dead! They didn't cut off your head at the plantation."

I laid Benny back in his bed and promised to come again soon.

Matthew and I hurried back to the plantation. About halfway there, we heard a group of men shouting drunkenly. It was a patrol looking for slaves who were away from their owners without written permission. We hid behind a large tree. We were thankful that they hadn't brought dogs with them. We rushed back to the plantation and were safely there before the morning horn called the slaves to work.

# CHAPTER 8

Miss Fanny, who had paid $50 for Grandmother's freedom, often came to Grandmother's house for afternoon tea. When she visited, Grandmother spread her table with a white cloth and used her best china cups and silver spoons. She served Fanny homemade muffins, delicate biscuits, and delicious cakes. Grandmother loved Fanny. The two women would sit together, sewing and chatting. Sometimes when they talked about old times, their eyeglasses would become dim with tears; they'd have to take them off and wipe them. When it was time to say goodbye, Fanny always left with a bag of Grandmother's best cakes and an invitation to come again soon.

A month after I'd left Grandmother's house, Fanny came to the plantation. She pretended that she'd come to see her grandnephew, Mr. Flint. Her real reason was to see how I was being treated. "Is there anything I can do to help you?" she asked.

"I don't think so."

"I'll never feel at peace as long as you and all of your grandmother's family are alive."

Each time that I traveled the twelve miles to and from Grandmother's house, I made plans to escape with Benny and Ellen.

After six weeks on the plantation, I asked Mr. Flint for permission to spend Sunday with Grandmother. He said yes.

On the way to Grandmother's house, I visited the slave graveyard. It was almost night. Only the occasional flutter of a bird broke the stillness. I knelt at my parents' graves. My father's was marked by a small wooden board; his name had worn away. I prayed to God to guide and support me in my planned escape. I had decided to hide at the house of my friend Louisa for a few weeks, until the Flints stopped searching for me.

I spent that Sunday at Grandmother's house, thinking that this might be the last day that I ever would spend there, talk with Grandmother, and be with Benny and Ellen. I knew the terrible future that my pretty Ellen would face as a slave. I was determined to save her from such a fate or die trying.

I started packing my things. Grandmother came into the room and said, "What are you doing?"

"I'm putting my things in order," I said,

trying to look cheerful.

Grandmother looked at me closely. "Harriet, do you want to kill me by trying to run away? Do you plan to leave your helpless children behind? I'm old now. I can't take care of Benny and Ellen the way I once took care of *you*."

"If I go away, Sands might be able to buy their freedom."

"Oh, my child, don't trust him. Stand by your children. Suffer with them until death. Nobody respects a mother who abandons her children. If you leave them, you'll never have another moment of happiness. If you go, you'll make me miserable for the few years I have left to live. If you run away, they'll capture you and bring you back. Remember how Ben was punished? Give up this plan, Harriet. Try to bear things a little longer. Things may turn out better than we expect."

For Grandmother's sake, I promised to try a little longer.

The next day I returned to the plantation. On Wednesday Mr. Flint's bride, Isabel, arrived. The other slaves expected little presents from their new mistress and hoped that things would be better under her rule. I had no such hopes. I knew that young wives often thought that cruelty was the best way to establish and keep their authority. Isabel Flint was young, attractive, and delicate-looking. She seemed excited by hopes for a bright future. She examined the entire house and told me that she was delighted with my preparation. I did my best to please her because I feared that Cora Flint would try to turn her against me.

That night I served dinner to George and Isabel Flint and their guests, including Dr. and Mrs. Flint. Cora Flint clearly was pleased to see me humbled. When I served her, she smiled triumphantly and didn't speak to me. Dr. Flint ordered me here and there, emphasizing the words "your mistress."

The next day, Isabel Flint took charge of the household. That night the slaves received their weekly allowance of food. Women received half the allowance of men. Children over twelve received half the allowance of women. Isabel Flint watched carefully. A very old slave, who had faithfully served the Flint family for three generations, limped up to get his bit of meat. Isabel Flint said, "He's too old to have a food allowance. When niggers get too old to work, they should be fed grass."

A week later a gentleman visited Mr. Flint, who showed him the wonderful cotton crop that had been grown by unpaid, poorly clothed, half-starved men and women. The gentleman admired the cotton and took some samples to show his friends. I was ordered to bring him water so that he could wash his hands.

The gentleman, who always had been friendly toward Grandmother and our family, asked me, "How do you like your new home, Harriet?"

"As well as I had expected."

"Oh. They don't think that you're happy. That's why tomorrow they're going to bring your children here to be with you. I'm sorry that you're unhappy. I hope that they'll treat you kindly."

The Flints were going to bring Benny and Ellen to the plantation! Why? I reasoned that they wanted to discourage me from trying to escape and wanted to break the children in. If I no longer was at the plantation, the Flints would have no reason to take Benny and Ellen away from Grandmother. I decided to run away that night.

After midnight I started sneaking down the stairs. I quietly opened a living room window and jumped out. The night was very dark, and large drops of rain were falling. Slowly I found my way to the road. Once there, I rushed toward Edenton.

A faithful friend named Sally was living at Grandmother's house. I tapped softly on her window. She woke up and opened the window.

I whispered, "Sally, I've run away. Let me in. Quick."

Sally opened the door softly and said quietly, "For God's sake, don't try to run away. Your grandmother is trying to buy you and the children. Mr. Sands was here last week. He said he was going away on business, but he told your grandmother to try to buy you. He promised to help her as much as he could. So don't run away, Harriet."

"Sally, they're going to take Benny and Ellen to the plantation tomorrow. Dr. Flint has said many times that he never will sell me. Knowing that, do you still advise me to go back?"

"No, child. No. When they find that you're gone, they won't want to be bothered with Benny and Ellen. But, Harriet, are you going all alone? Let me ask your Uncle Phillip to help you."

"No, Sally. I don't want to place anyone else in danger."

"Where will you hide? Dr. Flint knows every inch of this house."

"I have a hiding place. Will you take all my clothes out of my room and hide them in yours? That way, when George Flint and the sheriff come to search my room, they'll think that I've taken my things and run away."

Sally promised to do as I asked.

I couldn't leave without looking in on Benny and Ellen. I bent over the bed in which they slept. Then I knelt and prayed for them. After kissing them lightly, I hurried away. I ran, through the darkness and rain, to Louisa's house.

Early the next morning George Flint came to Grandmother's house. "Have you seen Harriet?" he asked Grandmother.

"No. I thought she was at the plantation."

Flint watched her face closely, to see if she was lying. "Don't you know anything about her running away?"

"I assure you, I don't."

"Last night she ran away for no reason. We had treated her very kindly. My wife liked her. We'll soon find her and bring her back. Are her children here with you?"

"Yes."

"I'm glad to hear that. If her children are here, she can't be far away. When she's brought back, her children will live with her on the plantation. If I find out that any of my niggers had anything to do with this damned business, I'll give them five hundred lashes."

Flint left to tell his father. The news made Dr. Flint storm and curse. Dr. Flint and his son searched Grandmother's house from top to bottom. Thanks to Sally, they found my room empty of clothing and assumed that I had left Edenton. Every northbound ship was thoroughly searched, and all passengers were read the law against protecting runaway slaves.

A special patrol watched Edenton that night. Everyone who went in or out of Grandmother's house was closely watched.

The Flints spent the next day searching for me. By the end of the day, the following notice appeared in every public area for miles around:

> **$300 REWARD! Ran away from her owner, Dr. Thomas Flint. An intelligent mulatto girl named Harriet, age 21. Five feet, four inches tall. Dark eyes. Black hair that tends to curl but can be straightened. Has decayed spot on a front tooth. She can read and write. Will probably try to get to the Free States. No one, under penalty of the law, is allowed to hide or employ this slave. $150 reward to anyone who captures her in North Carolina. $300 reward to anyone who captures her out of the state and either delivers her to me or holds her in jail.**
>
> **Dr. Thomas Flint**

# CHAPTER 9

The search for me lasted much longer than I'd expected. I was extremely anxious about placing Louisa at continued risk.

I managed to exchange messages with my family, who had been harshly threatened. They advised me to return to George Flint, ask his forgiveness, and let him make an example of me. I couldn't follow their advice.

One night about a week later, the searchers came so close that I thought they must have tracked me to my hiding place. I hurried from Louisa's house and hid in some thick bushes. I remained there for two hours in an agony of fear. Suddenly I felt something grab my leg. I hit it to loosen its hold. Pain soon told me that I'd been bitten by a poisonous snake.

Slowly I made my way back into Louisa's house. The pain had become intense. Louisa tried to treat the bite, but the swelling didn't subside. My family and friends knew that something had to be done right away, but where could they turn for help?

Mrs. Wright was a lady in town who had known Grandmother for years and always had been very friendly to her. She also had taken a kind interest in my mother, Willie, and me. Mr. and Mrs. Wright owned many slaves but always treated them well.

Having heard about my escape, Mrs. Wright visited Grandmother. "Do you know where Harriet is, Aunt Martha? Do you know if she's safe?"

Grandmother shook her head.

"You can trust me, Aunt Martha. Tell me all about it. Maybe I can help you."

Grandmother looked closely at Mrs. Wright. Something about the look on her face made Grandmother feel that she could trust her. She told her everything.

Mrs. Wright sat thinking. Then she said, "I'll hide Harriet for a while. But first you must solemnly promise that my name never will be mentioned. If anyone found out that I was involved, my family would be ruined. No one in my house must know of it, except Betty, our cook. Betty is so faithful that I'd trust her with my life. And I know that she likes Harriet. It's a terrible risk, but I believe that no harm will come of it. Get word to Harriet to be ready tonight, as soon as it's dark and before the patrols start their watch. I'll send the housemaids out on errands. Then

I'll have Betty go meet Harriet." She explained exactly where I was to meet Betty.

Grandmother was so grateful and relieved that she sank onto her knees and sobbed.

I received a message to leave Louisa's house at a specific time and go to a certain place, where a friend would be waiting for me. As a precaution, no names were mentioned. I didn't like taking such a blind risk, but I had no choice.

At the specified time I disguised myself and went to the meeting place. There I found my friend Betty. We hurried along in silence. My leg hurt so much that I thought I'd faint, but fear gave me strength.

We reached the Wrights' house and entered unobserved. Betty said, "Honey, now you're safe. Those devils won't come to search *this* house."

Mrs. Wright came to meet us. She led me upstairs to a small room above her bedroom. "You'll be safe here, Harriet. I use this room for storage. The housemaids never come here. They won't suspect anything unless they hear noise. I always keep this room locked. Only Betty has a key. You must be very careful, for my sake as well as yours. You must never tell my secret; that would ruin my family. Every morning I'll keep the housemaids busy, so that they won't see Betty bringing you your breakfast and treatment for your leg. After that, Betty won't be able to come back to you until night. I'll come to see you sometimes. Keep up your courage. I hope that this won't last long."

Mrs. Wright hurried downstairs. My heart overflowed with gratitude. Betty brought me a nice hot supper and treated my leg.

When I went to sleep that night, I felt that I was the luckiest slave in Edenton. The next morning I noticed that the swelling in my leg had begun to subside. My little room was filled with light from a small window. I was able to stay safely hidden while looking out onto the street below. I saw Dr. Flint going to his office.

Dr. Flint jailed Willie, Benny, Ellen (who was only two years old), and Aunt Nancy, who had faithfully served the Flints for twenty years. He told Grandmother that she wouldn't see them again until I was brought back. When I heard that Benny and Ellen were in that horrible jail, I wanted to rush to their rescue.

Mrs. Wright tried to reassure me that my aunt would take good care of Benny and Ellen while they were in jail. It was painful to think that my aunt was imprisoned for the "crime" of loving me.

I received a message from Willie:

Dear Sister,

I beg you not to come to the jail. We are much better off than you are. If you come, you will ruin all of us. They would force you to tell where you had been and who had helped you. If you refused, they would kill you. Take my advice—for the sake of your children and me, and for the sake of the friends who have helped you.

Poor Willie! I took his advice.

After a month, Cora Flint became tired of managing her household. It was much too tiring to order her meals and eat them, too. So she took Aunt Nancy out of jail and brought her back to her house.

Some time later, Ellen was taken out of jail. She had developed measles right before she was jailed, and her eyes still were affected. Dr. Flint brought her to his home to treat her. Ellen cried all day, begging to be taken back to prison. In jail she at least was loved.

Ellen's screams and sobs annoyed Cora Flint so much that finally she ordered one of her slaves to carry Ellen back to jail. "I can't stand this brat's noise. I hope the doctor will sell those children as far as wind and water can carry them. As for their mother, she'll find out what happens to slaves who run away. When she's caught, she'll be chained in jail for six months. Then she'll be sold to do hard labor on a sugar plantation. That good-for-nothing slut! I'll see her broken in yet. Now hurry up and take that brat back to jail. And don't let any niggers in the street speak to her."

Early the next morning, Dr. Flint went to see Grandmother. "I thought I'd just stop by and tell you that I've learned where Harriet is hiding," he lied. "I'll have her in my hands by noon."

Grandmother sent a message to Betty. Not wanting to alarm Mrs. Wright, Betty took care of the matter herself. She sneaked me into the kitchen, locked the door, and lifted a floorboard. Underneath was a small space where she had placed a rug for me to lie on and a quilt to cover me.

Betty said, "Stay there until I find out if the Flints really know that you're here. If they come searching among my things, they'll get one blessed sassing from *me*!"

When Betty was alone in the kitchen, I heard her cursing the Flints. Every now and then, she chuckled and said, "This nigger's too clever for them this time."

When the housemaids came into the kitchen, Betty found clever ways to get them to tell what they'd heard about me. She also suggested places I might have gone.

One housemaid said, "She isn't stupid enough to stay around here. She must be in Philadelphia or New York by now."

After everyone else was asleep, Betty lifted the floorboard and said, "Come out, child. They don't know anything about you. It was only white folks' lies, to scare the niggers."

A few days later I had a worse fright. I was sitting quietly in my little room when I heard a voice that chilled my blood: Dr. Flint's. I was sure that Flint had come to seize me. I looked around in terror. There was no way to escape. Then the voice faded. Flint and the sheriff must be searching the house.

A little later, I heard footsteps approaching. A key turned in my door. I crouched in terror. When I looked up, there stood Mrs. Wright.

"I thought you'd hear your master's voice," she said. "I knew that you'd be terrified, so I came to tell you that there's nothing to fear. In fact, you might laugh at the reason that he came to see me. He thinks you're in New York, and he came to borrow travel money. My sister loaned him $500, on interest. He's leaving tonight, so you're safe for now."

Dr. Flint returned from New York, having spent much money without, of course, finding me. He also had to pay to keep Willie, Benny, and Ellen in jail. It had been two months now, and he felt discouraged.

Sands thought it might be a good time to get Dr. Flint to sell Willie, Benny, and Ellen, so he sent a slave trader to offer $900 for Willie and $800 for the two children. Although these amounts were above the going rate, Flint asked for more: $1,900. The trader agreed. He paid Flint the money, the bill of sale was signed, and Willie, Benny, and Ellen were in the trader's hands.

An hour after the sale, Flint went to the trader and said, "Sir, I must ask you not to sell any of those slaves within North Carolina. Otherwise, you'll have to pay me an additional $1,000."

"You're too late," the trader said. "Our deal is closed." He didn't tell Flint that he already had sold Willie to Sands and the children to Grandmother.

Sands had given Grandmother the money to buy Benny and Ellen, but he didn't want anyone to know this. Among white Southerners, a gentleman who buys the freedom of his enslaved children is regarded as a traitor who has damaged the system of slavery. Because Grandmother was free, Sands was able to have the children's bill of sale drawn up in her name.

When Willie, Benny, and Ellen arrived at Grandmother's house, there was great rejoicing.

The next morning, I heard two housemaids in the kitchen. One said to the other, "Did you know that Harriet Jacobs's children were sold to a trader yesterday? I expect their daddy bought them. They say that he's bought William, too."

When Betty came, I anxiously told her what I'd heard. Grinning broadly, she said, "Mr. Sands has bought William, Benny, and Ellen. I have to laugh, thinking about old Dr. Flint. Lord, how he'll rant! I'd better get out of here before those housemaids spot me." Betty went off, laughing.

I thought, "Can it be true? Thank God!"

People were surprised to find out that Benny and Ellen were with Grandmother. The news spread throughout Edenton.

Dr. Flint went to Grandmother and demanded, "Who bought the children?"

She answered, "Arthur Sands."

"I thought so. Don't expect to ever see *Harriet* free. She'll be my slave as long as I live. When I'm dead, she'll be my children's slave. If I ever find out that Phillip had anything to do with her running off, I'll kill him. If I run into

William in the street and he dares to look at me, I'll beat him within an inch of his life. And keep those brats out of my sight!"

# CHAPTER 10

Dr. Flint had Uncle Phillip arrested. Uncle Phillip was charged with having helped me to run away, and I feared that he would be found guilty of a crime. No court of law would accept the word of a black over that of a white. In court Uncle Phillip truthfully swore that he hadn't known anything about my intention to escape and hadn't seen me since I left George Flint's plantation. Dr. Flint demanded $500 in bail before he'd allow Uncle Phillip to be released. Several gentlemen offered to pay the $500. Sands arranged for Uncle Phillip to be released without bail.

Dr. Flint started another search for me. Betty again hid me under the kitchen floor. After everyone was asleep, she came to release me. My fear, the damp ground, and the position I'd been forced to stay in made me ill for several days.

I already had stayed at the Wrights' house longer than intended. Friends kept trying to plan my escape, but the Flints were watching so closely that it was impossible to make a move.

One morning, I was startled by the sound of someone trying to get into my room. Several keys were tried in the lock, but none fit. When Betty came up to see me, I told her what had happened.

"I know who it was," she said. "I'm sure it was that housemaid Jenny. That nigger has the devil in her."

"Do you think that Jenny has seen or heard anything?"

"No, child. She only *suspects* something. She saw the new dress that you made for me, and she wants to know who made it. She won't ever know."

"Betty, I must leave here tonight."

"Do as you think best, poor child. I *am* afraid that Jenny might find out you're here."

Betty told Mrs. Wright what had happened, and Mrs. Wright instructed her to keep Jenny busy in the kitchen.

Mrs. Wright went to talk with Uncle Phillip, who said that he would send a friend for me that evening. Mrs. Wright said, "I hope that Harriet is going to the Free States. It's very dangerous for her to stay anywhere nearby."

Taking Jenny with her, Mrs. Wright spent the rest of the day visiting her brother in the countryside. She was afraid to come say goodbye to me, but she had Betty convey her kind wishes. I never saw this generous woman again.

That evening I had no idea where I was going  Betty brought me a sailor's outfit. She told me to put it on, put my hands in my pockets, and walk like a sailor. She said, "I'm so glad you're going to the Free States! Don't forget me." I started to thank her for her kindness, but she interrupted me. "I don't want any thanks, honey. I'm glad I could help you. May the good Lord protect you."

Betty walked with me to the Wrights' gate. A young black man named Peter, who had learned carpentry from my father, was waiting for me. I had known Peter many years. He always had been kind. Betty said goodbye, and Peter and I walked away.

"Take courage, Harriet," Peter said. "I've got a knife. No man will take you from me unless he does so over my dead body."

I prayed that Peter wouldn't have to use his knife. It had been a long time since I'd walked outside. The fresh air enlivened me. It also was pleasant to have someone speak to me above a whisper.

When Peter and I reached the shore, Aunt Nancy's husband, David, was waiting for us with a rowboat. Peter and I got in, and David rowed us some distance out from shore. We waited there until just before dawn. Then

David rowed us about three miles, to a swamp. Peter and I were to hide there until Uncle Phillip had prepared a hiding place for me.

Peter got out of the boat and, using a large knife, cut a path through bamboo plants and prickly vegetation. He made a seat among the bamboos. Then he came back to the boat, took me in his arms, and carried me to the seat. Before we reached it, we were covered with hundreds of mosquitoes.

As daylight increased, I saw snakes crawling all around us—the largest I'd ever seen. I was terrified. At twilight there were so many snakes that Peter and I had to keep beating them off with sticks.

The bamboos were so high and thick that we couldn't see any distance. Just before dark, we moved closer to the swamp's entrance, so that we would be able to find our way back to the rowboat.

Finally we heard the movement of oars and a low whistle, which was David's signal. Peter and I hurried into the boat, and David rowed away from shore. The swamp's heat, numerous mosquito bites, and constant fear of snakes had given me a fever, so I had trouble falling asleep.

I had just fallen asleep when Peter and I had to return to the swamp. This time Peter burned tobacco to keep mosquitoes away.

The smoke nauseated me and gave me a severe headache.

At dark we returned to the boat. David said that I would be hidden in Grandmother's house.

"How is that possible?" I said. "Dr. Flint knows every corner of that house."

"Wait and see," David said.

David rowed Peter and me back to Edenton, and Peter and I walked into the town. I had blackened my face, and I still was wearing the sailor's outfit. I passed several people whom I knew. At one point, Sands was so close that I brushed against his arm. No one recognized me.

"You must make the most of this walk," Peter said sadly. "You may not have another soon."

Attached to Grandmother's house was a small storage shed that opened, on one side, onto a courtyard. The shed had a sloped roof covered with thin shingles. The sloping space between the shed and its roof was a sort of attic nine feet long, seven feet wide, and three feet high at its highest point. The attic had no openings for light or air. While I was hiding in the swamp, Uncle Phillip had made a hidden trapdoor between the shed's storeroom and attic.

As soon as I entered Grandmother's house, I was taken to the shed's attic. The air was stifling; the darkness was complete. I lay down on blankets that had been spread on the floor. If I turned from one side to the other, I hit the sloping roof. Although rats and mice scurried over me, I soon fell asleep.

Without any light, day and night were the same. I knew it was morning when I heard voices outside. It was horrible to sit or lie in a cramped position day after day. Yet, I knew slaves who suffered worse fates. Some had their heel tendons cut so that they couldn't run away. Some were chained to logs and forced to drag them around while they worked in the fields, from morning to night. Some were branded with hot irons.

At least, I could talk with Grandmother, Uncle Phillip, and Aunt Nancy through the trapdoor and hear my children's voices. At night Grandmother passed food up to me. It was impossible to stand up, so I crawled around for exercise.

One day I hit my head on something. It was a small drill that Uncle Phillip had forgotten to take with him after completing the trapdoor. That night I crawled to the attic's street side and drilled a hole about one square inch. I sat by this hole until late that night, enjoying the whiffs of air that entered.

The next morning, I watched for Benny and Ellen. The first person I saw in the street was Dr. Flint. I shuddered. At last I heard the merry laughter of Benny and Ellen. Soon their sweet little faces looked up in my direction. I longed to tell them that I was there.

For weeks hundreds of tiny red insects tormented me. Their bites made my skin burn. The attic's heat was intense. Nothing but thin shingles protected me from the scorching summer sun.

Aunt Nancy brought me all the news that she heard at Dr. Flint's house. Flint wrote to a black woman from Edenton who now was living in New York. He offered her a reward if she could find out anything about me. Soon after, he went to New York.

When Flint passed by Grandmother's house the morning after his return, Benny happened to be standing at the gate. Benny had heard people say that Flint had gone away to find me, so Benny ran to him and asked, "Dr. Flint, did you bring my mother home? I want to see her."

Flint answered, "Get out of the way, you damned rascal! If you don't, I'll cut off your head!"

Benny said, "You can't put me in jail again. I don't belong to you now," and ran into the house.

I told Grandmother about the incident and begged her not to let Benny and Ellen say things to Flint that might prompt him to harm them.

Autumn brought some relief from the heat. My eyes had become used to dim light. By holding a book or needlework close to the peephole, I managed to read and sew.

In winter Grandmother brought me extra blankets and warm drinks. It was so cold that many days I had to lie in bed, wrapped in blankets. My shoulders and feet became frostbitten. On warmer days, I'd sit, wrapped in blankets, at the peephole.

People often stopped to chat on the street below, so I heard many conversations. I heard slave hunters plan ways to catch runaway slaves. I heard talk about Dr. Flint, my children, and me. One person said, "I wouldn't lift my little finger to catch her because she'd have to go back to old Flint." Another responded, "I'd catch *any* nigger for the reward. A man has a right to keep what belongs to him, even if he *is* a damned brute." I heard many people say that I must be in the Free States. Almost no one suggested that I might be anywhere nearby. If anyone had suspected that I was in Grandmother's house, it would have been burned to the ground.

One day Dr. Flint took Benny and Ellen into a store and offered to buy them some shiny little toys if they would tell him where I was. Ellen shrank from him and wouldn't speak. Benny said, "Dr. Flint, I don't know where my mother is. I guess she's in New York. When you go there again, please ask her to come home. I want to see her. But if you put her in jail or tell her you'll cut her head off, I'll tell her to go right back."

When Christmas was approaching, Grandmother brought me materials to make some clothes and toys for Benny and Ellen. I had the pleasure of seeing my children through the peephole when they went into the street wearing their new clothes. Benny asked one of his little playmates, "Did Santa Claus bring you anything?"

"Yes," the boy answered. "I got presents. But Santa Claus isn't a real man. It's children's mothers who bring them things."

"That's not possible," Benny said. "Ellen and I got these new clothes. Santa Claus must have brought them because my mother's been gone a long time."

I longed to tell Benny that his mother *had* made his clothes and that many tears had fallen on them while she worked.

I was warned to keep extremely quiet during Christmas dinner because Grandmother had invited two guests. When I heard the guests talking in the courtyard, my heart almost stopped beating. One was a free black man who tried to pass himself off as white and who betrayed other blacks. This man had spent many nights hunting for me. The other guest was Edenton's sheriff. Most slave owners looked down on him because he was too poor to own slaves. He had to content himself with whipping any slave he caught outside after 9:00 p.m.

Grandmother had invited these two men to convince them that she had nothing to hide. All the rooms in her house were open. She took the men to different parts of the house, pretending to show them different things that she'd collected. Grandmother sent them home with some pudding.

When spring came, I could see a little patch of green through my peephole. I longed to breathe fresh air, stretch my cramped legs, stand upright, and feel the earth beneath my feet.

In summer the attic was, once again, stifling. When it was extremely hot, I welcomed thunderstorms because their rain came through the roof and cooled the attic's hot boards. However, in cooler weather, storms that soaked my clothes left me feeling chilled.

I heard and saw many things that reminded me why I was hiding. One Edenton slave named Alice gave birth to a child who looked just like her master. When the master's wife saw the baby, she threw Alice and her baby out of doors and told her never to return. Alice went to her master, the baby's father, and told him what had happened. He promised to take care of everything. He sold Alice and her baby to a slave trader from Georgia.

Another time, I saw a slave woman rush wildly past Grandmother's house. Two men were chasing her. Her mistress had ordered her to be stripped and whipped because she had made some minor mistake. The woman ran down to the river, jumped in, and put an end to her misery.

Such horrors are common in every Southern state, yet Senator Brown of Mississippi told the U.S. Congress that slavery is "a great moral, social, and political blessing—a blessing to the master and a blessing to the slave."

In the winter, cold and lack of movement made my legs cramp and go numb. My face and tongue stiffened so much that I couldn't speak. Willie tried to doctor me. At one point, I lost consciousness for sixteen hours. I returned to consciousness when Willie splashed cold water in my face. Then I became delirious. Willie drugged me so that I wouldn't cry out in my feverish state. I stayed in bed for six weeks.

One day a child's screams made me crawl

out of bed. From my peephole I saw that Benny was covered with blood. A fierce dog, usually kept chained, had attacked him. Benny screamed as a doctor sewed his wounds. It was a long time before Benny could walk again.

Then Grandmother fell ill. I longed to take care of her. A number of her regular customers visited her with little gifts and wishes for her recovery. Aunt Nancy asked Cora Flint for permission to spend a night looking after Grandmother. Mrs. Flint replied, "I don't see why you have to go to her. Besides, I need you here." Then Mrs. Flint learned that a number of ladies had visited Grandmother. Because she didn't want to seem less Christian than they, she went to see Grandmother.

Surprised to find Grandmother so ill, Mrs. Flint immediately sent for her husband. Dr. Flint came, declared Grandmother in critical condition, and said that he would be happy to doctor her. Grandmother declined the offer. She didn't want him coming to the house or sending a large bill for his services.

As the Flints were leaving, Mrs. Flint noticed that Benny still was limping from the dog attack. "I'm glad the dog attacked him," she said. "I wish he'd been killed. It would be good news to send to his mother. Her day will come. The dogs will grab her yet."

Soon after, Grandmother began to recover.

# CHAPTER 11

That summer, Sands ran for Congress. Although Dr. Flint belonged to the same political party, he campaigned for Sands's defeat. In an effort to buy votes against Sands, Flint threw large parties at which he provided plenty of rum and brandy.

Sands was elected. Soon he would leave for Washington, D.C. What if something happened to him while he was away? If he died, could his heirs claim Benny and Ellen as their property, even though the bill of sale was in Grandmother's name? Years had passed since I'd spoken to him.

The night of Sands's departure, I sneaked down from the attic into the storeroom—so stiff that I barely could move. My ankles gave way, and I sank to the floor. I crawled to the window and waited, hidden behind a barrel, hoping that Sands would visit Grandmother. The clock struck nine. I knew that his boat would be leaving between ten and eleven. My hopes were fading. Then I heard his voice. He said to someone, "Wait here a minute. I want to see Aunt Martha."

After Sands spoke with Grandmother, he passed by the storeroom window. I whispered, "Stop here one minute. Let me speak for my children."

Startled, he stopped for a moment, then went out through the gate. I sank down behind the barrel, in despair.

A few minutes later he returned. "Who called me?"

"I did."

"Harriet, I knew your voice, but I was afraid to answer. I didn't want my friend to hear. Why have you come here? Why would you risk your life by being in this house? They're crazy to let you be here."

I didn't want to involve him in the danger, so I didn't tell him that I was hiding in the attic. "I came here to speak to you about Benny and Ellen. Many things could happen during your six months in Washington. Before you go, please ensure that Benny and Ellen are free, or authorize some friend to do that."

"I will. I'll also try to buy *you*."

I heard footsteps approaching, so I quickly closed the window. I tried to crawl back to the attic, but I had no more strength.

Grandmother found me in the storeroom. She called Uncle Phillip, who carried me back up.

When I'd lived in the attic nearly five years, I decided that I needed to stand up straight and exercise my limbs. Otherwise, I might be crippled for life. Early one morning, before anyone was out on the street, I went down into the storeroom and restored warmth and feeling to my limbs through exercise. I started doing this every day.

I missed Willie, who had gone to Washington with Sands. Sands had promised to give Willie his freedom, but he hadn't set a time.

Willie sent Grandmother several letters. After some time, Sands wrote that Willie had proven himself a faithful servant and valued friend. They had traveled together through Northern states and into Canada. Sands said that they'd be home soon.

We expected letters from Willie, describing his travels. None came. Then we heard that Sands would be coming home late in the fall, with a wife.

The day of Sands's scheduled return, Grandmother set a place for Willie at the dinner table. The stagecoach passed the house, but it was empty. Grandmother waited a while longer to serve dinner. Perhaps Willie had been delayed.

Sands sent word to Grandmother that Willie hadn't returned with him. Grandmother cried as if she'd heard of Willie's death rather than his freedom. She was afraid that she'd never see him again.

I, too, thought more about what I'd lost than about what Willie had gained. Now I had more reason to worry about Benny and Ellen. If Sands resented losing money on Willie, he might be less willing to ensure their freedom, especially now that they were old enough to be valuable property. Also, now that Sands was married, his feelings about them might change.

Finally Grandmother received a letter from Willie. He wrote that Sands always had been kind to him, but ever since childhood he had longed to be free. "When I have earned enough money to give you a home, I hope you will come north. There we can all live happily together."

Sands told Uncle Phillip, "I trusted William. I met him as he was leaving our hotel, carrying his trunk. I asked him where he was going, and he said that he was going to replace his old trunk. I offered to give him some money for a new one. He said, 'No thank you,' and walked away. When he didn't return, I looked to see whether he had packed our trunks for the trip home. He'd left a note. It said that he hoped God would bless and reward me for my kindness but that he wanted to be free. I had intended to give him his freedom in five years. He might have trusted me. Instead, he's been ungrateful. I won't go after him, though. I'm confident that he'll soon return to me."

When Dr. and Mrs. Flint heard that Willie had run away, they had a good laugh about Sands. Mrs. Flint said, "I'm glad of it. I like to see people get what they deserve. I reckon that he'll make Harriet's children pay for William's freedom. I'd be glad to see them in a slave trader's hands. I'm tired of seeing those little niggers running around the streets."

One day, when Sands and his wife were walking in the street, they saw Benny. Mrs. Sands immediately liked him. She said, "What a pretty little Negro! Who owns him?"

Sands told his wife that he was the father of Benny and Ellen and that they were motherless. A few days later, Sands asked Grandmother to bring Benny and Ellen to him. Mrs. Sands wanted to raise Benny in her home. Her sister, a childless woman who was visiting from Illinois, wanted to adopt Ellen.

I sent Grandmother to tell Sands that Benny and Ellen were *not* motherless, and to remind him of his promise to ensure their freedom.

Surprised by my message, Sands told Grandmother, "The children are free. Harriet may decide their future. In my opinion, they would be better off in the North. I don't think they're safe here. Dr. Flint claims that they still belong to his daughter. He says they were sold when she was still a child, so the sale wasn't legally binding."

The Sandses wanted to take Ellen to Washington, D.C. and keep her with them until they could arrange for friends to bring her to Mr. Sands's cousin, Mrs. Hobbs, in Brooklyn. The Sandses promised that Mrs. Hobbs would take good care of Ellen and send her to school. I gave my consent.

Mrs. Sands had just had a daughter. She probably would be happy to have a slave woman's child to help take care of her baby. I didn't like the idea of Ellen being a maid to her half sister—even temporarily—but I felt that Ellen's journeying to Washington and then Brooklyn was the best option.

The night before Ellen was to leave, I sneaked into my old room in Grandmother's house. I hadn't seen it for more than five years. Uncle Phillip came in, leading Ellen by the hand. I put my arms around her and said, "Ellen, I'm your mother."

She stepped back a little and looked at me. Then she let me hug her.

I said, "I've loved you all the time that you haven't seen me. Now that you're going away, I wanted to see you and talk to you."

With a sob, Ellen said, "I'm glad that you've come to see me. Why didn't you ever come before? Benny and I have wanted to see you. Why didn't you come home when Dr. Flint went to get you?"

"I couldn't come before. Are you glad to be going away?"

"I don't know," she said, crying. "Grandmother says that I'm going to a good place, where I'll learn to read and write. But I won't have anybody to love me. Can't you go with me? Please, Mother!"

I took her in my arms. "I'm a slave. That's why I can't go with you and why you mustn't ever say that you've seen me. God will see that you make friends. Be a good child. Try to please the people in your new home. Always say your prayers. Someday God will let us be together. You, Benny, and I will live together and be happy."

That night, Ellen and I stayed in my bedroom. She slept, and I watched her sleep.

Before dawn I had to return to the attic. I bent over Ellen and hugged her close. She woke up, wept, and kissed me one last time. She whispered, "Mother, I'll never tell."

Later that morning I heard the gate close behind Ellen. When Dr. and Mrs. Flint learned that Sands had taken Ellen away, they were quite upset. Mrs. Flint said, "Admitting that he's the father of those little niggers shows that Sands has no respect for either his wife or his own character. And taking the girl is stealing from us! When Emily is twenty-one, she'll get both children."

Months passed with no news of Ellen. I wrote to Mrs. Hobbs. She wrote back that Ellen hadn't come to her yet. I wrote to Sands in Washington. He didn't answer. I was becoming suspicious. Sands certainly wouldn't be the first congressman to deceive others with regard to his mulatto children. I once saw a letter that a congressman wrote to a woman who was his slave and the mother of six of his children. He said that he was going to bring some friends from Washington home with him. He wanted the slave woman to keep their children out of sight. He didn't want his friends to see that the children looked like him. He wasn't ashamed of having had six children by his slave; he only was afraid that his friends might find out.

After six months, Grandmother received a letter from Mrs. Hobbs's young daughter, who wrote that Ellen had just arrived. "She is a nice girl. We will enjoy having her with us. Mr. Sands has given her to me, to be my little maid. I will send her to school. I hope that someday she will write to you herself."

This letter confused and upset me. Had Sands sent Ellen to Brooklyn only until she was able to support herself as a free woman, or did he regard her as property?

# CHAPTER 12

Aunt Nancy had married David when she was twenty. Dr. and Mrs. Flint had allowed her to marry, and a minister had performed the ceremony.

As a wedding present, Mrs. Flint provided a small room that Aunt Nancy and David could share when David, a sailor, wasn't at sea. But on her wedding night, Aunt Nancy was ordered to sleep in her usual place, on the floor outside Mrs. Flint's bedroom. At the time, Mrs. Flint was expecting a child. What if she should want a drink of water in the middle of the night? What would she do without her slave to bring it to her?

Even after Aunt Nancy became pregnant, she was forced to sleep on the floor and get up whenever Mrs. Flint summoned her. Aunt Nancy gave birth, prematurely, to a stillborn baby. Two weeks later, Mrs. Flint gave birth, and Aunt Nancy was required to breast-feed the infant.

Aunt Nancy had five more stillborn children. Broken by hard work and lack of sleep, she almost died. Afraid of losing a valuable servant, the Flints finally allowed her to sleep in her own room except when they needed her to care for someone who was ill. Aunt Nancy gave birth to one infant who lived a few days and another infant who lived about a month.

After my mother died, Aunt Nancy was like a mother to Willie and me. Whenever others discouraged me from running away, Aunt Nancy encouraged me. All the years that I hid in the attic, Aunt Nancy visited me whenever she could. She always tried to comfort and cheer me. The whole family relied on her wisdom and advice.

One day, after I'd lived in the attic for six years, Grandmother was called to Dr. Flint's house. Aunt Nancy had suffered a severe stroke. The Flints allowed Grandmother to sit at her bedside. Aunt Nancy had lost the ability to speak, but mother and daughter looked at each other lovingly.

Two days later Aunt Nancy died. Mrs. Flint was so overcome that she took to her bed. With moist eyes, Dr. Flint said, "We'll never be able to replace her."

While Grandmother was sitting beside her dead daughter, Dr. Flint said, "I'd like to forget about the past, Martha. I'd like Harriet to come and take over Nancy's duties. She would be worth much more to us working here than anything we could sell her for. I wish it for your sake, too. Now that Nancy is gone, having Harriet nearby would be a great comfort to you."

When Uncle Phillip told me that Aunt Nancy was dead, I was overwhelmed with grief.

Mrs. Flint had overworked Aunt Nancy for years, slowly murdering her. Yet, she now asked her minister if she could bury Aunt Nancy in the graveyard in which she herself would be buried. Only whites had been buried there. All members of my family were buried in a graveyard for slaves. The minister said, "I don't object to going along with your wish, but Aunt Martha may have her own thoughts about where to bury her daughter."

When asked, Grandmother immediately said, "I want Nancy to lie with the rest of our family."

Mrs. Flint honored Grandmother's wish but said, "I find it painful to have Nancy buried away from *me*." After all, she was used to sleeping with Aunt Nancy nearby on the floor.

The Flints gave Uncle Phillip permission

to pay for the funeral. Slave owners always are ready to do *that* kind of favor for slaves and their relatives. It was a simple but respectable funeral. Mrs. Flint's minister read the funeral service. Many blacks came, both enslaved and free, as well as a few whites who had been friendly with our family. Mrs. Flint actually shed a tear at the gravesite.

# CHAPTER 13

On New Year's Day my friend Annie was sold to one master, and her four little girls were sold to another, far away. Annie escaped. They searched her mother's house, which was next door to Grandmother's. The slave hunters came so close to me that I was afraid to leave the attic. Soon after, Benny happened to see Annie in her mother's house. He told Grandmother.

I had lived in the attic for almost seven years when Peter came to tell me, "Your day has come, Harriet. There's a chance for you to go to the Free States on a ship headed north. It leaves in two weeks. Will you go?"

I was about to answer with a joyful "yes" when I thought of Benny. "How can I leave Benny behind?"

"Such a chance might never come again. Benny is free and can be sent to you in the North. For your children's sake, you must go."

Uncle Phillip was delighted with the plan and urged me to go. He promised that he'd bring or send Benny to me.

When I was ready to leave, my family received horrible news about an Edenton slave named Jim. After an especially severe whipping, Jim had run away into the woods and hidden there, half-naked and starving. After several weeks he'd been found, tied, and brought back to his master's plantation. The overseer had whipped him until he was cut from head to foot. Then Jim had been washed with saltwater and placed in a cotton gin, which was screwed down until it pressed on his ripped flesh. In the gin, Jim had enough room only to lie on his back or side. His master intended to leave him there for several weeks. On the first morning, a slave placed a piece of bread and a bowl of water on the floor near Jim. On the second morning, the bread was gone, but the water hadn't been touched. For four days the slave left bread and water. On the fifth day, the slave told his master that the water hadn't been touched and that a horrible smell was coming from the gin. When the gin was unscrewed, the overseer saw Jim's dead, decaying body. Rats must have eaten the bread placed near the gin. Jim was hurriedly buried in a box. No one asked any questions.

Hearing about Jim revived Grandmother's worst fears about my being captured. She begged me not to go. I, too, became afraid. I promised to give up the escape plan.

When I told Peter, he said, "How can you throw away such a rare chance?"

I suggested that Annie take my place on the ship, and Peter agreed.

Annie's mother was surprised that we knew Annie's secret but overjoyed that her daughter had a chance to escape. One night Annie was carried onboard and hidden in a small cabin. Because she was a runaway, the price paid for her to sail a few hundred miles equaled the price of a voyage to England.

For three days, stormy weather kept the ship from leaving. On the fourth day, Grandmother asked me to come down into the storeroom. She was so worried that Annie would be discovered, and we all would be in danger, that she started sobbing.

Someone outside the shed called, "Where are you, Aunt Martha?"

Without thinking, Grandmother opened the door. In stepped Jenny, Mrs. Wright's mean-spirited housemaid. "I've been hunting everywhere for you," Jenny said. "My missus wants you to send her some crackers."

I had hidden behind a barrel. Grandmother immediately realized what she'd done. She quickly stepped outside with Jenny and locked the door behind her.

Grandmother returned a few minutes later, frantic. "My carelessness has placed you in great danger. The ship isn't gone yet. Get ready immediatcly. Go with Annie!" Grandmother and Uncle Phillip agreed that if Jenny had seen me, she probably would tell Dr. Flint as soon as she finished her day's work.

Although I hated to place Peter in more danger, I asked him for help. He immediately went to the wharf. The ship had just left. He gave two boatmen a dollar apiece to take him to the ship.

The captain saw the boat coming toward his ship. Because the boatmen were white and Peter's skin was even lighter than theirs, the captain thought that law officers were pursuing his ship in search of Annie. The captain increased his ship's speed, but Peter's boat gained on the ship. When Peter reached the ship, he jumped aboard. The captain recognized him, and they went below deck to speak privately.

"There's another woman I want to bring onboard," Peter said. "She's in great danger. Please stop and take her! I'll pay you any amount within reason."

The captain agreed to wait at a certain place, where I could sneak onboard after dark.

I decided to spend the little time that I had left with Benny. I had watched him through my peephole, but not spoken to him, for seven years. Grandmother brought Benny to the shed and locked us in. We talked and cried.

Benny said, "Mother, I'm glad you're going away. I wish I could go with you. I knew you were here. I've been so afraid that they would come and catch you."

I was surprised. "How did you know I was here?"

"One day I was standing outside when I heard somebody cough above the storeroom. I don't know why I thought it was you, but I did. The night before Ellen went away, I noticed that she wasn't in her bed. When Grandmother brought her back into our room before dawn, she whispered to Ellen, 'Remember never to tell.'"

"Did you ever tell Ellen that you thought I might be hiding over the storeroom?"

"No, but if I saw her playing with other children on that side of the house, I always tried to get them to move to the other side. I was afraid they might hear you cough. I tried to keep a close lookout for Dr. Flint. If I saw him speak to the sheriff or a patrol, I always told Grandmother."

Now that I thought about it, I had seen Benny look uneasy when people outside our family had been near the shed. Although Benny was only twelve, he already was cautious and alert.

"Now I really *am* going to the Free States," I said. "If you're a good, honest boy and love Grandmother, the Lord will bless you and bring you to me. Then you, Ellen, and I will live together."

Grandmother walked in and gave me a small bag of money. I begged her to keep some of it, at least to pay for Benny's trip north. Weeping, she insisted that I take it all.

I went up to my attic for the last time. I felt new hope, but I was sad to leave Grandmother's house forever.

When it was time to leave, I went down into the storeroom. Grandmother and Benny were there. Grandmother took my hand and said, "Harriet, let us pray." We knelt. With one arm I pressed Benny to my heart. With the other I embraced Grandmother, who prayed for mercy and protection.

Peter was waiting for me in the street. I was weak in body but strong in purpose. My brain was whirling, and I repeatedly stumbled. Somehow Peter and I reached the wharf. There we met Uncle Phillip, who had arrived earlier to make sure that it was safe. Two sailors in a rowboat were waiting for us.

As I was about to step into the rowboat, someone pulled me gently. I turned and saw Benny, looking pale and anxious. He whispered, "I've been watching Dr. Flint's window. He's at home. Don't cry. I'll come to you soon." He hurried away.

I squeezed Uncle Phillip's hand, and Peter's. We parted in silence. Our hearts were too full for words.

The rowboat glided swiftly over the water. One of the sailors said, "Don't worry, Ma'am. You'll get safely to your husband in Springfield." I realized that the captain must have told his crew some false story.

When I boarded the ship, the captain came out to meet me. He was an elderly man with a pleasant face. He showed me to a tiny cabin. There sat Annie. When I entered, she jumped. She stared at me in disbelief. "Harriet! Is it really you?"

We held each other, and I sobbed.

The captain kindly reminded us that we mustn't attract attention, for his safety as well as ours. "Please stay in the cabin whenever there's another ship in sight. At other times you're welcome to come on deck. I'll keep a sharp lookout. I don't think you'll be in danger if we act cautiously. I told my crew that you're going to meet your husbands in Springfield, Illinois."

Annie told me how much she had suffered and how terrified she had been while hiding in her mother's house. But she talked most about the agony of having her children taken from her.

The ship soon set sail. The wind was against us, so we moved slowly. Until miles of water separated us from our enemies, Annie and I were terrified that the sheriff or slave hunters would come onboard. The captain already had been paid for our trip. What if he tried to make even more money by turning us over to slave hunters?

Annie comforted me. "I've already spent three days onboard, while the ship was docked in Edenton. No one betrayed me. Everyone has treated me kindly."

Soon the captain suggested that we go on deck for some fresh air. He was so friendly and respectful that I felt reassured. He offered us some comfortable chairs. He told us that he had been born in the South and had spent most of his life there. His brother, who recently had died, had been a slave trader. "Slave trading is a miserable business. I always was ashamed that he was involved in it."

I'll never forget that night. The spring air was so refreshing. And when we sailed into

Chesapeake Bay in broad daylight, the brilliant sunshine and invigorating breeze filled me with joy.

Ten days after we had set sail, we approached Philadelphia. The captain said, "We'll arrive in port during the night. I think that you ladies should wait until morning to leave the ship. People will be less suspicious if you go on shore in broad daylight."

The next morning, for the first time in our lives, Annie and I saw the sun rise over free land. We looked at each other with tears of joy in our eyes.

The sailors rowed Annie and me over to the dock. I shook their strong hands, with tears of gratitude in my eyes.

I never had seen such a big city. As I stood looking around at Philadelphia, the captain said to me, "There's a respectable-looking black man standing behind you. I'll tell him that you want to go to New York and ask him about trains."

A few minutes later the captain introduced Annie and me to Reverend Jeremiah Durham, who took my hand as if I were an old friend.

Reverend Durham said, "You're too late for the morning trains to New York. You'll have to wait until this evening or tomorrow morning." Assuring me that his wife would welcome me warmly, he invited me to go home with him and invited Annie to stay with one of his neighbors. I thanked him.

Annie and I said goodbye to the captain. We told him that we'd always be grateful for his help. I asked him if he would deliver a message to my family, and he promised that he would.

Mrs. Durham greeted me in a kind, friendly way. She didn't ask me any questions.

After dinner Reverend Durham spoke with me privately. He asked about Ellen because I had mentioned that I was going to meet her. I suspected that he would ask me next about my husband. I told him the truth about Benny and Ellen, even though I feared that he'd lose respect for me.

When I finished, he said, "Excuse me if my questions have pained you. I wanted to understand your situation so that I can help you and your little girl. I respect you for answering me honestly, but don't answer everyone so openly. Some people might use your past as an excuse to treat you with disrespect."

Mrs. Durham entered the room. She said that an antislavery friend had come to the house and would like to see me.

The friend asked me many questions about my experiences and my escape, but she was careful not to say anything that might hurt my feelings. The Antislavery Society was going to pay for Annie's trip to New York. They offered to do the same for me. I said that my grandmother had given me enough money to cover my travel expenses.

Mrs. Durham, who was much better educated than I was, took me out to see some of Philadelphia. One day we went to an artist's studio where she showed me portraits of her children. I never had seen paintings of blacks before. They were beautiful.

After five days in Philadelphia, Reverend Durham took Annie and me to the train station and handed us our tickets. "I'm afraid that you'll have an unpleasant ride. I couldn't buy you first-class tickets."

Thinking that I hadn't given him enough money, I offered more.

"Oh, no. No matter how much you're willing to pay, blacks aren't allowed to ride in the first-class cars."

That was my first experience of racial prejudice in the North. In the South, black train passengers had to sit in a filthy boxcar behind the cars holding whites, but they didn't have to pay for the privilege.

On the train, Annie and I sat in a large car crowded with people of different races and nationalities. The windows were so high that we had to stand to look out of them. Babies kicked and screamed. People told coarse jokes and sang crude songs. Half the men smoked cigars or pipes. Jugs of whiskey were passed around. The whiskey fumes and thick tobacco smoke made me feel sick.

# CHAPTER 14

When Annie and I arrived in New York, she went to a home that the Antislavery Society had provided for her. Later I would hear that Annie had found a good job.

I headed to the Brooklyn home of Judy, a black woman who was from Edenton and had known my parents. Judy lived near Ellen. Just as I was about to knock on Judy's door, two girls passed me on the street. I recognized the older girl. She was Sarah, the daughter of a woman who once had lived with Grandmother. I hugged her and asked how her mother, Rachel, was doing.

Then I looked more closely at the younger girl. It was Ellen! I pressed her to my heart and then held her at arm's length to look at her. She had changed a lot in the two years since she'd left home. Anyone could see that she'd been neglected. I thought that we would all go inside, but Ellen said, "I'm on an errand. As soon as I finish it, I'll go home and ask Mrs. Hobbs to let me visit you tomorrow."

Sarah hurried off to tell Rachel that I was in Brooklyn. The same day, Rachel and other friends from Edenton visited me at Judy's house. They questioned me eagerly, laughed, and cried. They thanked God that I had escaped.

The next day, Ellen came with a message from Mrs. Hobbs inviting me to her house. In her note Mrs. Hobbs assured me that I had nothing to fear.

But my conversation with Ellen troubled me. When I asked Ellen if Mrs. Hobbs treated her well, she replied with a halfhearted yes. Ellen had been living with Mrs. Hobbs for two years. Sands had said that Ellen would go to school. Now, at age nine, Ellen barely knew the alphabet. There was no excuse for this. Brooklyn had good public schools that Ellen could attend for free.

Ellen stayed with me until dark. Then we went to the Hobbses' house. Before we went inside, Ellen said, "Mother, when will you take me to live with you?" It made me sad that I couldn't give her a home until I could find work and earn enough to pay rent.

The Hobbs family received me in a friendly way. Everyone said that Ellen was a good, useful girl. Mrs. Hobbs looked me coolly in the face and said, "I suppose you know that my cousin, Mr. Sands, has given her to my oldest daughter. When Ellen grows up, she'll be a nice maid for her."

I didn't say anything. Now I understood why the Hobbses had kept Ellen uneducated. To them, she was nothing but a servant.

When I returned to Judy's house, I wrote a polite letter to Dr. Flint. I asked how much money he wanted for me. Because I legally belonged to his daughter Emily, I wrote to her as well, asking the same question.

I tried to find out about Willie. I heard that he'd been in Boston. When I went there to look for him, I learned that he'd gone to New Bedford, Massachusetts. I wrote there and was told that he'd gone to sea on a whaling ship and wouldn't return for several months. I returned to Brooklyn, to try to find work near Ellen.

I received a discouraging letter from Dr. Flint. He advised me to return and give myself up. If I did, he'd grant any request that I might make.

I applied for jobs, but every potential employer wanted a reference. One day an acquaintance told me that a white Manhattan couple, Charles and Lilly Bruce, wanted a live-in nurse for their baby. I immediately applied for the job.

Mrs. Bruce asked me many questions. To my relief, she didn't require a recommendation from a former employer. I was pleased to learn that she was from England because I'd heard that the English were less racially prejudiced than Americans. Mrs. Bruce hired me for a month's trial period.

Before the month was over, my legs were so painfully swollen from the frequency with which I went up and down stairs that I couldn't perform my duties. Many women would have fired me without another thought, but Mrs. Bruce arranged my duties so that I didn't have to walk as much. She also paid a doctor to look after me.

Mrs. Bruce noticed that I often was sad and asked me why. I told her that I missed my children and other relatives who were dear to me. I didn't tell her that I was a runaway slave. I had lost all trust in whites.

After six months with Mrs. Bruce, her gentle manner and the lovely smiles of her baby, Mary, began to thaw my chilled heart. Mrs. Bruce's intelligent conversation widened my mind, as did my freedom to read whenever I had time off from my duties.

Mrs. Bruce said that Ellen could come live with me, but I was afraid of offending the Hobbses and what they might do as a result. When Ellen visited me, she usually brought a note from Mrs. Hobbs asking me to buy Ellen a pair of shoes or some clothing. Mrs. Hobbs always promised to pay me back as soon as her husband received his paycheck. Somehow payday never came. I had to spend much of my earnings to keep Ellen adequately clothed.

Ellen still suffered from eye inflammation. Mrs. Bruce suggested that Ellen come to Manhattan for a while. She would arrange to have Ellen treated by an eye specialist. When I asked Mrs. Hobbs to send Ellen to me for medical care, she angrily refused.

One morning I noticed a young man in a sailor's outfit walking down the street and looking into every house that he passed. Could it be Willie? I opened the front door and called to the sailor. In less than a minute I was wrapped in Willie's arms. We laughed and cried. We had so much to tell each other.

# CHAPTER 15

Emily Flint didn't answer my letter asking her to sell me. After a while, I received a letter written by Dr. Flint (I recognized his handwriting and style). He pretended that the letter had been written by Emily's younger brother. The letter urged me to come home. If I did, the Flints would greet me "with open arms and tears of joy" and sell me to anyone I chose. I didn't bother to reply.

Soon after, I received a letter from a Southern friend telling me that Dr. Flint was about to come north. I told Mrs. Bruce that I had an important matter to take care of in Boston. Mrs. Bruce agreed to let me have a friend take my place for two weeks.

I left right away for the Boston residence of my friend Melanie. As soon as I arrived, I wrote to Grandmother asking her to send Benny to Melanie's address as soon as possible. Grandmother had the legal power to do that because her name was listed on the bill of sale as Benny's legal owner. Grandmother sent Benny on a ship that sailed directly to Manhattan, where a friend met him, took him to see Ellen in Brooklyn, and then sent him on to Boston.

Early one morning there was a loud knock at Melanie's door. In rushed Benny, out of breath. "Oh, Mother, here I am! I ran all the way, and I came all alone. How are you?"

I was overjoyed.

Benny chattered away as fast as his tongue could go. "Mother, why don't you bring Ellen here? I went to Brooklyn to see her, and she felt very bad when I said goodbye. She said, 'Oh, Benny, I wish I was going, too.' I thought she'd have learned a lot already from going to school, but I can read and *she* can't. Here in the North, I suppose free black boys can do anything that white boys do."

Dr. Flint came to New York but failed to find out where I was. His family, who were waiting for me "with open arms," must have been quite disappointed.

As soon as I heard that Flint had returned south, I left Benny in Willie's care. I returned to the Bruces' home and stayed there through the winter and spring. I found much happiness in Mrs. Bruce's kindness, Mary's affection, and Ellen's occasional visits.

When summer came, the Bruces and I traveled to northern New York State. On the steamboat, Mrs. Bruce invited me to accompany her to the dining room for afternoon tea and feed Mary there. I told her that I'd feed Mary but that I preferred to sit alone with Mary. "I'm afraid of being insulted."

Mrs. Bruce said, "You won't be insulted if you're with *me*."

We went to the dining room and saw several white nurses enter with their ladies. They all were treated properly. But as soon as I sat down, someone said harshly, "Get up! You're not allowed to sit here." To my surprise and indignation, the person ordering me to leave was black. Even if he had to enforce the ship's rules, he might have done so politely.

I said, "I won't get up unless the captain himself comes and takes me away."

The waiters didn't offer me a cup of tea, so Mrs. Bruce handed me hers and then ordered another cup.

The next morning the Bruces and I stopped for breakfast at a restaurant in a small city. Mrs. Bruce said, "Take my arm, Harriet. We'll go in together."

The restaurant's owner heard her and said, "Madam, will you allow your nurse and baby to have breakfast with my family?"

I knew that this was a way for him to keep a black woman from sitting at the breakfast table with white ladies. But because he had asked politely, I complied.

At our lakeside resort, I found myself surrounded by Southerners. I looked around, terrified of seeing someone who would recognize me. I was delighted that we didn't stay there long.

We returned to Manhattan for a few days, before going to spend the rest of the summer at a seaside hotel in Rockaway, New York. I went to Brooklyn to see Ellen and happened to meet her in front of a grocery store, where she was running an errand.

Ellen said, "Oh, Mother, don't go to Mrs. Hobbs's house. Her brother, Mr. Thorne, is visiting from the South. He might tell where you are."

I thanked her for the warning and said that I'd try to see her as soon as I got back from Rockaway.

On the train to Rockaway, I was allowed to ride in the white car, but only because I was the servant of a white family. The Bruces and I stayed in a large, fashionable hotel. Some of the ladies had black maids and coachmen. However, although there were thirty or forty other nurses of various nationalities, I was the only black one.

When it was time for tea, I took Mary and followed the other nurses. A young man pointed me to a seat at the end of a long table.

Because there was only one chair, I sat down and took Mary in my lap. The young man immediately came up to me and said coolly, "Will you please seat the little girl in the chair? You may stand behind the chair and feed her. Afterward, you will be shown to the kitchen, where you may eat your meal."

All the other nurses glared at me. Although their skin was only one shade lighter than mine, they looked at me as if I were contaminating the table. I hardly could control my anger, but I said nothing. I quietly took Mary in my arms, went to our room, and refused to go back to the table.

Mr. Bruce asked the hotel to send meals for Mary and me to our room. The hotel's waiters, who were white, soon complained that they hadn't been hired to wait on blacks. For this reason, the hotel's owner asked Mr. Bruce to send me back to the dining table.

Then the black servants of the other hotel guests were unhappy because *I* was allowed to eat at the dining table and *they* weren't. I think they should have refused to submit to such treatment. After all, the hotel charged the same amount for black servants as for white ones. Because I stood up for my rights, I ended up being treated well.

# CHAPTER 16

$A$s soon as the Bruces and I returned to Manhattan, I went to see Ellen. She never complained about her troubles and always looked out for my safety.

One day I insisted on knowing why she looked so sad. Finally she said, "Mr. Hobbs and Mr. Thorne drink a lot. Sometimes they're so drunk that their hands tremble and I have to pour their liquor for them. They often send me to the store for rum and brandy, and I'm ashamed to ask for liquor so often. But Mr. Hobbs is good to me. I feel sorry for him and can't help liking him."

Thorne was reckless and poor. In the South he often went to blacks to borrow money or get a good dinner. He never asked such favors of whites, whom he considered his equals. I tried to avoid seeing him, but Mrs. Hobbs said that he wanted to see me. "He is sorry that you seem to be avoiding him. He knows that you're living in Manhattan. He told me to tell you that he owes thanks to 'good old Aunt Martha' for many little acts of kindness and never would be base enough to betray her grandchild."

When I visited, Thorne greeted me in a very friendly way. He said, "I congratulate you on your escape and hope you've found a good place where you're happy."

One Sunday afternoon late in October, Ellen was anxiously waiting for me outside the Hobbses' house. "Oh, Mother, I've been waiting so long to see you! I'm afraid that Mr. Thorne told Dr. Flint where you are. Hurry up and come inside. Mrs. Hobbs will tell you all about it."

The day before, Ellen had been sweeping the yard while the Hobbs children were playing outside. Thorne had come out with a letter in his hand. He had torn it into pieces and left them on the ground. Suspicious, Ellen had picked up all the pieces and asked the children if they would read the letter to her. They did. The letter said, "I have seen your slave Harriet. If you are careful, you can take her easily. There are enough of us here to identify her as your property. I am a patriot; I love my country. I do this out of respect for the law." The letter informed Flint of my address.

The children had taken the letter to Mrs. Hobbs, who immediately had gone to her brother's room for an explanation. Thorne hadn't been there. The servants had told Mrs. Hobbs that they'd seen Thorne leave with a letter in his hand. Mrs. Hobbs had reasoned that the torn letter must be an earlier version of some final message to Dr. Flint.

When Thorne had returned, Mrs. Hobbs had accused him of betraying me, and he hadn't denied this. That night, he had left the Hobbses' house.

I hurried back to Manhattan. That evening Mrs. Bruce saw how upset I looked and asked me why. I told her my full story. She said, "I'll do everything I can to protect you."

The next morning, Mrs. Bruce consulted a lawyer and a judge. They advised me to leave New York City immediately. If I was arrested, I probably would have to go back with Dr. Flint.

Mrs. Bruce arranged for me to stay at the Manhattan home of one of her friends. She assured me that I'd be safe there. Mrs. Bruce instructed her servants to tell anyone who asked about me that I used to live with her but no longer lived in Manhattan.

I pleaded with Mrs. Hobbs to let Ellen come to me. Mrs. Hobbs gave in but said that Ellen must return within ten days. I avoided making any promises. Ellen came to me wearing thin, outgrown clothes. Knowing that she must be cold, I took off my flannel skirt and cut and sewed it to fit her.

Mrs. Bruce came to say goodbye and noticed that I had used my skirt to clothe Ellen. Tears came to her eyes. She said, "Wait for me, Harriet," and hurried from the house. She soon returned with a nice warm coat for Ellen.

Willie came to Manhattan to take Ellen and me to Boston. We reached the steamboat safely. Mrs. Bruce's lawyer met us there and tried to ensure that we would be treated well. So many wealthy people traveled on this boat that blacks weren't allowed to stay in cabins. I was afraid to stay on the open deck because it was very cold and because someone might recognize us. I took Ellen by the hand, went to the captain, and politely asked if he could arrange for us to sleep somewhere other than on deck. He said that it was not the usual custom but that he would arrange for us to stay in a room. He also offered to try to get us comfortable train seats for the next part of our trip. I don't know whether Ellen's sweet face had won his heart or Mrs. Bruce's lawyer had urged him to take care of us, but I was surprised and grateful to receive so much kindness. Everyone treated us properly, and we reached Boston safely.

My first day in Boston was one of the happiest of my life. I felt that I was beyond the reach of slave hunters. For the first time in many years, I had both Benny and Ellen with me. The children laughed and chatted merrily.

New York City was unsafe, so I accepted Melanie's offer to share her residence and expenses. I earned some money by sewing.

I told Mrs. Hobbs that Ellen had to stay with me so that she could get an education. Ellen felt ashamed that she still couldn't read or spell. Instead of sending her to school with Benny, I taught her myself until she had learned enough to attend school.

The winter passed pleasantly. I was busy with my needle, and Benny and Ellen were busy with their books.

In the spring I received sad news. Lilly Bruce was dead. I had lost an excellent friend, and Mary had lost a loving mother. Mr. Bruce wanted to take Mary to visit some of her mother's relatives in England, and he asked me to go with them to take care of Mary. I thought that Mary would be happier with me than with a stranger. Also, my income would increase if I went. So I agreed. Ellen would stay with Melanie and go to school, and Benny would become an apprentice and learn a trade.

After a pleasant voyage, Mr. Bruce, Mary, and I arrived in England. There, for the first time in my life, I was treated with full respect.

As I lay my head on my pillow the night that we arrived, I had my first delightful feeling of pure, complete freedom.

I had heard much about the hard lives of poor people in England, but I found that the poorest, least educated English people were better off than the best-treated slaves. English people worked hard, but they never were forced to work under threat of a whipping. Their homes were simple, but no patrolmen could enter them in the middle of the night and abuse the occupants. No man, however rich and powerful, was free to violate women or take children from their parents. No law forbade anyone to learn to read and write.

Mr. Bruce, Mary, and I stayed in England ten months, which was much longer than I had planned. During all that time I never saw the slightest hint of racial prejudice.

Upon my return to the United States, I hurried back to Boston. Ellen was doing well and making progress in school. Benny wasn't there to welcome me. For several months his apprenticeship had gone well. The master and the other apprentices had liked him. Then they'd discovered that Benny was a "nigger." The other apprentices had started to insult and abuse him. Benny had too much self-respect to accept such treatment, so he'd taken a job on a whaling ship. When I heard this news, I wept and blamed myself for having been away so long.

Then I received a letter from Dr. Flint's daughter Emily. She wrote, "I have married Daniel Dodge and now am independent of my father. Mr. Dodge and I will be moving to Virginia, and I would like you to come and live with us. I always have felt close to you." She asked me to return to Edenton and signed the letter "your friend and mistress." I didn't reply. I felt safe in Massachusetts, where no law required the return of a runaway slave and opposition to slavery was strong.

# CHAPTER 17

For two years Ellen and I lived comfortably in Boston. Then Willie offered to send Ellen to a boarding school in Rochester, New York. It was hard for me to part with her, but I accepted Willie's generous offer.

The night before Ellen was to leave, I said, "Ellen, I have something to tell you." I told her how I had suffered as a slave and said, "I want you to know about your father."

"I know all about it, Mother. I'm nothing to my father, and he's nothing to me. I spent five months with him in Washington. He never cared for me at all. He never spoke to me the way he did to his little girl, Maggie. I knew all the time that he was my father. Maggie's nurse told me so. She said that I mustn't ever tell anybody, and I never did. I used to wish that he would take me in his arms and kiss me the way he kissed Maggie. I wished that he would at least smile at me. I thought that, because he was my father, he should love me. I was just a little girl then; I didn't know any better. Now I don't even think about my father. All my love is for you."

The next morning Willie took Ellen to Rochester. Soon after, I received a letter from Willie asking me to join him in Rochester. He wanted to start a business selling paper goods and antislavery literature. I went, and we opened the shop.

For a year I lived with the family of Isaac and Amy Post. Amy and Isaac were Quakers and true believers in human equality. Amy worked to end slavery and gain equal rights for women.

The shop started by Willie and me failed because there wasn't enough antislavery feeling in Rochester to support it. Willie decided to go to California. He and I agreed that Benny should go with him.

Ellen liked her school and was highly regarded there. When the school accidentally discovered that I was a runaway slave, they lowered her tuition and helped her in other ways.

In need of a job, I went to see Mr. Bruce. Mary was growing into a tall girl, and Mr. Bruce had remarried. Although his new wife, Gertrude, was from a wealthy American family, she showed no racial prejudice. She despised slavery. From the moment I met her, I liked her. Because she had just given birth, she and Mr. Bruce asked me to stay with them and be the baby's nurse. I agreed.

Soon after, the Fugitive Slave Law went into effect. This law made it a federal crime to help a runaway slave. Even people living in the Free States had to obey this law. No one who had escaped from slavery was safe.

Black families who had lived in New York City for twenty years now fled the city. Poor laundry women who had made a simple home for themselves through years of hard work had to give up all their furniture, quickly say goodbye to their friends, and start over in Canada. Many husbands and wives learned that their spouse was a runaway who must leave. Because the children of slave mothers are considered slaves, fathers suddenly discovered that their beloved children could be taken from them and carried into slavery.

The Fugitive Slave Law didn't apply to Willie because he had left his master in a Free State, but it applied to me because I had run away from a Slave State. Whenever I had to run an errand for Mrs. Bruce, I tried to avoid busier streets so that I wouldn't encounter anyone who might recognize me.

One day I recognized Luke, a slave who had belonged to Mr. Rogers, a wealthy, cruel Edenton man. Rogers had become so drunkenly that he rarely got out of bed. Every day, he would order Luke to bare his back and kneel beside the bed. Using a leather rope that he kept beside him, Rogers would whip Luke. If he ran out of strength, he would summon the sheriff to continue the whipping. Eventually, Rogers had started making Luke do sick, disgusting things. I was thrilled to see that Luke had escaped from slavery.

I told Luke about the Fugitive Slave Law and asked, "Do you have enough money to get to Canada?"

"You can depend on it. I'd worked all my life for those accursed whites, and the only pay I'd ever received was kicks and whippings. So when Rogers died, I took some of his money and put it inside a pocket of one of his old pants. After Rogers was buried, I asked his kin for those pants, and they gave them to me." He chuckled. "You see, I didn't steal the money. They *gave* it to me." Luke soon went to Canada.

All that winter I lived in fear. In the spring an Edenton friend warned me that Dr. Flint knew I had returned to the Bruces' home. Flint was making plans to come and capture me.

I told Mrs. Bruce about my danger. She immediately arranged for me to go to New Hampshire, and she insisted that I take her baby, Olivia, with me. "It's better for you to have Olivia, Harriet. That way, if they find you, they'll have to bring Olivia back to me. Then I'll know where you are, and if there's any chance of saving you, we will."

Mrs. Bruce had a wealthy uncle who supported slavery. He objected to her sheltering a runaway slave. "You're breaking the law," he said to her. "Are you aware of the penalties?"

"Yes. Imprisonment and a thousand-dollar fine. Shame on this country for passing such a law! I'm ready to take the consequences. I'd rather go to prison than have some poor soul taken from my house and dragged back into slavery."

In New Hampshire I was sheltered by a senator and his wife. The senator was strongly opposed to the Fugitive Slave Law. From the senator's house I went into the countryside, where I hid with Olivia for a month.

When Dr. Flint seemed to have given up looking for me, I returned to the Bruces' home.

Several months later, Grandmother sent me a letter: "Dr. Flint is dead. Poor old man! I hope that he has made his peace with God." I felt much less forgiving than Grandmother.

Dr. Flint's death didn't lessen my danger. Flint had left almost nothing for his children. Cora Flint told her daughter Emily that she couldn't afford to lose such valuable property as I was.

One night I learned that Emily Dodge and her husband had arrived in Manhattan. They were staying in a cheap hotel. Because I never had seen Mr. Dodge, I wouldn't recognize him if he came to look for me. At that very moment he might be waiting outside to capture me.

I hurried to tell Mrs. Bruce, who quickly called for a carriage. Mrs. Bruce put a dark veil over my face, placed Olivia in my arms, and got into the carriage with me. We drove all around, turning and retracing our path so that no one could follow us. Finally we stopped at the house of one of Mrs. Bruce's friends, who sheltered me. Mrs. Bruce immediately returned home to tell her staff what to say if anyone asked for me.

Soon after, a man came to the Bruces' house and asked for me. A short time after, another man came. He brought a letter from Grandmother, which he said he needed to deliver directly to me.

Each man was told, "She used to live here, but she left."

"How long ago?"

"I don't know, Sir."

"Do you know where she went?"

"No, Sir." And the door was closed.

The next morning, Mrs. Bruce came to me and begged me to leave the city. She said that her house was being watched. Once again, I fled to New Hampshire with Olivia.

Several days later Mrs. Bruce sent me a letter: "Mr. Dodge still is searching for you. I intend to end your torment by buying your freedom."

I wrote back, "Thank you, but I can't accept your kind and generous offer. Being sold would reduce me to property."

Without my knowledge, Mrs. Bruce hired someone to negotiate with Mr. Dodge. The negotiator offered Dodge $300 if he would give up all claim to my children and me. At first, Dodge laughed at the offer. It was so little money.

The negotiator said, "Do as you choose, Sir. If you don't accept this offer, you'll never receive anything for the woman. She has wealthy friends who will sneak her and her children out of the country."

Deciding that something was better than nothing, Dodge agreed to the offer.

The next day, Mrs. Bruce wrote to me, "I rejoice to tell you that Mr. Dodge has been paid for your freedom. I have seen the bill of sale. Come home. I long to see you and Olivia."

My head spun as I read her letter. "The bill of sale." I had been sold like a piece of merchandise. At the same time, a heavy load was lifted from my weary shoulders. Riding back on the train, I no longer was afraid to take off my veil and look at other people.

When I reached the Bruces' house, my generous friend threw her arms around me. We both wept.

Mrs. Bruce said, "Oh, Harriet, I'm so glad it's over! You wrote that you felt your services were being transferred from one owner to another. I didn't buy you for your services. I would have done the same thing if you wanted to leave for California tomorrow. I just wanted you to be free, and now you *are*."

Grandmother lived long enough to rejoice in my freedom. But soon after, I received a letter with a black seal on it. At last, she was at peace.

Soon after, an Edenton friend sent me a newspaper notice of Uncle Phillip's death. I never had seen an obituary written about a black. One of Uncle Phillip's white friends had written, "Now that he has died, he is called a good man and a useful citizen. What good does such praise do a black man when his soul has left this world?" A "citizen." How strange to hear that in the South!

My story ends with freedom for me and my children. I pray that all who remain enslaved will soon be free.

# AFTERWORD

## About the Author

*Incidents in the Life of a Slave Girl* is an autobiography, the author's true story of her own life. But *Incidents* is a special type of autobiography known as a slave narrative. It focuses on Harriet Jacobs's experiences as a slave—mostly during her teens and twenties. To protect her family and friends, as well as other runaway slaves, Harriet changed their names and some of the details. But she wrote about what really happened to her, even though telling her story was often humiliating, terrifying, and painful.

Harriet Ann Jacobs was born in Edenton, North Carolina in 1813. Her parents, Delilah Horniblow and Daniel Jacobs, were both slaves, although they belonged to different owners. In some ways, young Harriet had a happier life than many slave children. Her parents' masters allowed them to live as a family, even though slaves could not be legally married. Until her mother died, Harriet's parents were allowed to raise Harriet and her brother, John (renamed William in the book), in a loving home. But as the child of a slave woman, Harriet legally belonged to her mother's mistress, Margaret Horniblow (renamed Ruth Nash in the book). Margaret Horniblow was kinder than most slave owners. She taught Harriet how to sew—a skill that later helped Harriet earn money to support her own two children. Margaret Horniblow also taught Harriet to read and write. Since it was against the law for slaves to teach each other to read, Harriet might have never learned if her mistress had not taught her.

Three sudden deaths destroyed Harriet's happy childhood. When Harriet was only six years old, her mother died. Six years later, her mistress died. In her will, Margaret Horniblow left Harriet to her niece, Mary Matilda Norcom (Emily Flint in the book). But since Mary was only three years old at the time, Mary's father, Dr. James Norcom (renamed Dr. Flint in the book), treated Harriet as his own slave. A year later, Harriet's father also died.

Now, at the age of only twelve, Harriet was left alone to fight off her master's sexual advances. How could she keep from being abused by Dr. Norcom? He was an important white citizen, a well-respected local physician, a wealthy and powerful man—and he owned her. He used the strength of his status, money, gender, and laws to try to force her into a sexual relationship. Harriet, an innocent and thoughtful young girl, was humiliated by Dr. Norcom's comments and frightened by his threats. Where could she turn for help? Should she confide in her grandmother, Molly Horniblow (Aunt Martha in the book)? Harriet knew that her grandmother had strong ideas about what was right and proper, and she was ashamed to tell her about the embarrassing and horrible things that Dr. Norcom said and did to her. Desperately looking for protection, Harriet turned to another powerful white man, a lawyer— Samuel Tredwell Sawyer (renamed Mr. Sands in the book). In 1829, when she was only sixteen years old, Harriet gave birth to their son, Joseph (Benny). Two years later, when she was 18, she bore their daughter, Louisa (Ellen).

While Harriet was trying to escape her master's abuse, other people were trying to end the entire system of slavery. White and black people worked together to help slaves escape from the South by hiding them in safe places, known as "stations" on the "underground railroad." Politicians in Washington, D.C., argued about the economics and morality of slavery.

Ordinary citizens known as "abolitionists" (because they believed that slavery should be ended or abolished), held meetings and wrote about the evils of slavery. In the same year that Harriet's daughter was born, Nat Turner, a slave, led a rebellion in Virginia. Tensions grew between slaves and their owners, between Northerners and Southerners, and even between members of the same family. Everyone felt threatened and afraid.

So, in 1835, Harriet took another desperate step toward freedom—not just for herself, but for her children as well. She hid in the small attic above her grandmother's storeroom. By doing this, she hoped to convince Dr. Norcom that she had run away, so that he would sell her children to their father, Mr. Sawyer. But in 1837, Mr. Sawyer was elected to the U.S. House of Representatives. He moved to Washington, D.C., but never legally freed their two children. Instead, he sent their daughter to Brooklyn, N.Y., where she was treated as a servant.

Desperate to rescue her daughter, Harriet finally left the South in 1842. After seven long years hiding in a tiny attic, Harriet sneaked onto a boat and went to New York City. There she found a job working for the wife of a writer named Nathaniel Parker Willis (Mr. Bruce in the book).

But Harriet never felt safe in New York City because Dr. Norcom kept looking for her there. So in 1849, she moved to Rochester, New York. There she worked with her brother in an antislavery bookstore and reading room. Just below their shop, Frederick Douglass published an antislavery newspaper, called *The North Star*. Harriet came to know Frederick Douglass, who had recently written and published a book about his experiences as a slave. His story became one of the most famous and popular of the over 100 published "slave narratives." In Rochester, Harriet also met and became close friends with Amy Post, an abolitionist and feminist. After hearing her story, Amy encouraged Harriet to write about her experiences, too. Amy wanted Harriet to show slavery from a woman's point of view and inspire other women to resist their abusive masters. Harriet Beecher Stowe had written *Uncle Tom's Cabin*, in which she described the life of slaves in the South. The book was very popular, especially among white women, who wept when they read this dramatic and emotional story. But Harriet Beecher Stowe was a white Northerner. She had only imagined the events in *Uncle Tom's Cabin*; she had not lived them herself. Amy Post encouraged Harriet Jacobs to write about what life was really like for a slave woman in the South. She tried to convince Harriet that her book might help abolitionists as well as other runaway slaves. But Harriet resisted the idea, explaining, "You know a woman can whisper her cruel wrongs in the ear of a dear friend much easier than she can record them for the world to read."

Other events kept Harriet from writing her book. In 1850, the Fugitive Slave Law made it a crime to protect runaway slaves, even in the "Free States." Northerners began to send runaway slaves back to their so-called rightful owners in the South. It was no longer safe to stay in New York. Harriet thought about joining her brother in California, where no one would know her—and no one would know that she was a runaway slave. Instead, Cornelia Grinnel Willis (Gertrude Bruce in the book), her employer's second wife, bought Harriet from the Norcom family in 1852. She then gave Harriet her freedom.

At last, Harriet began writing her autobiography. But she still found it humiliating to tell her story. As Harriet wrote, "It would have been more pleasant to me to have been silent about my own history." Would details of her sexual life offend white women? Would they be angry with Harriet for leaving her children behind, while she hid from her master? Northerners might think that Harriet's decisions were "immoral." What if the book hurt, rather than helped, the cause of other slave women? But Harriet kept working, even though she had to write secretly and late at night. She hid her book from Mr. Willis, who thought that black people would be happiest if they remained slaves. Working under such difficult conditions, it took Harriet years to complete her book. All day long, she had to take care of her employer's house and family.

By 1858, Harriet had finally finished a draft of *Incidents*. She asked Lydia Maria Child, a white woman who was famous for writing against slavery, to help her edit the book. Finding someone to publish it was even more of a challenge. At the time, female authors were expected to write romantic fiction about women who devoted their entire lives to their husbands and children. Who would publish a true story about a black woman who talked back to a wealthy white doctor, criticized the hypocrisy of the church, had two children as a single teenager, and chose to live independently of men? Harriet went all the way to England in search of a publisher, but she was not successful there, either. In 1860, she finally found a Boston publisher who accepted her book. Unfortunately, the company went out of business before they could do the job. But Harriet did not give up. Eventually she was able to buy the printing materials from the bankrupt publisher, and in January, 1861, she finally found someone to print copies of her book.

Harriet's book received good reviews in both the United States and in England. But a few months after *Incidents in the Life of a Slave Girl* was published, the Civil War broke out. The public's attention was focused on the war, and Harriet's book was largely forgotten.

Having published her story, Harriet turned her energies to helping black people, rather than writing books. In 1862, she and her daughter returned to the South. There they assisted people who had been displaced by the war. On January 1, 1863, President Abraham Lincoln's Emancipation Proclamation gave freedom to many slaves. But these freed slaves were left with nothing—no money, no skills, and no place to live. They desperately needed clothing, shelter, health care, and education. In 1863, Harriet and her daughter started the Jacobs Free School in Virginia, a school run by black people for black people. A year later, Congress ended the Fugitive Slave Law, which had terrified runaway slaves for thirteen years. In 1865, the Civil War was over. And in the same year, the Thirteenth Amendment to the Constitution put a final end to slavery in the United States.

Yet Harriet was still not safe. The laws had changed, but not everyone obeyed them. In the South, racists began terrorizing black people. In 1870, afraid for her daughter and herself, Harriet opened a boarding house in Massachusetts. Only in the mid-1880s did Harriet and her daughter move south again, this time to Washington, D.C. After spending all her life running away from violence and abuse, she was finally able to settle down in a place where she could feel both safe and free. Harriet Jacobs died in Washington, D.C., on March 7, 1897.

## About the Book

When *Incidents in the Life of a Slave Girl* appeared in 1861, it was the first full-length slave narrative written by a woman. Around the time of its publication, Harriet Jacobs explained her purpose in writing the book: to make "women of the North" realize that two million women in the South were "still in bondage, suffering what I suffered, and most of them far worse." But then the Civil War started, and few people had a chance to read *Incidents*. After the war was over, the book was almost forgotten. Slavery had been abolished in the United States, so what was the purpose of reading Harriet's book?

Then, in the 1960s and 1970s, *Incidents* was rediscovered, and a second edition was finally published in 1973. Why the renewed interest in a 100-year-old book? Civil rights activists and historians wanted to know more about the history of African Americans. *Incidents* showed how black and white people, men and women, slaves and free blacks, Northerners and Southerners, and old and young people had worked together for a common cause—sometimes to protect slaves and sometimes to oppress them. Supporters of women's rights and feminist scholars were interested in how women in the 1800s were exploited by men, and how they asserted themselves. They admired and were inspired by how Harriet Jacobs resists Dr. Flint and survives. Philosophers and religious reformers wanted to know more about the role of religion and spirituality in a slave-owning society. Why, they wondered, does Harriet continue to believe in God, even while she criticizes the hypocrisy of many Southern churches? People still read *Incidents* to understand more about slavery, the rights of women and minorities, and religion and ethics.

But people who are not activists or scholars also enjoy reading *Incidents*. They find that this book speaks to their lives, their problems, and their dreams. For this is the story of a young person's struggle for freedom and control over her own life. Despite the harsh limits that slavery sets on her, Harriet finds ways to make her own choices and to take responsibility for them. She chooses whom she will love. She takes responsibility for how she uses her own body. She decides where she can live and when she must leave. She controls what she says and writes. And, against overwhelming odds, she lives her life according to her own beliefs about what is right and what is wrong.

Harriet carefully determines whom she can respect and trust, and whom she cannot. One of the people she loves most is her "good old grandmother" who risks her own health and safety to hide Harriet and protect her children. Harriet knows that she can trust her "brave and generous friend" Peter, the "intelligent, hard-working, noble-hearted man" who helps her escape to the North. But she also recognizes who is not trustworthy, and soon learns that "no promise or written contract with a slave is legally binding." As an innocent young girl, Harriet trusts the kind words and attention of an "older and more powerful" man, Mr. Sands. But later, when she realizes that Mr. Sands has not kept his promise to free their children, she stops depending on him. That is when Harriet takes matters into her own hands. She finds her daughter, earns enough money to support her, and looks after Ellen's well-being herself.

As a slave, Harriet does not legally own her body. Yet she uses her body to regain some control over her life. She wants to be a virgin when she marries her true love. But she faces the fact that this young black man can never legally marry her or shelter their children from slavery. Harriet realizes that, sooner or later, she will be forced to give up her virginity to a white man. She chooses to have a sexual relationship with Mr. Sands, rather than allow her abusive master Dr. Flint to rape her. As distasteful as her decision is to her, she concludes that an active choice is preferable to becoming Dr. Flint's passive victim. During Harriet's pregnancy, she becomes so ill that her family and friends ask Dr. Flint to give her medical care. But preferring to die rather than let her would-be rapist touch her body, Harriet screams until he leaves the room.

To the best of her ability, Harriet decides where she will live. First as a slave girl and later as a runaway, Harriet is forced to move frequently. When her mother dies, she must leave her father and move into the Flints' house. As a six-year-old child, what choice does she have? But when Dr. Flint tries to force Harriet to live in an isolated cottage, where he can "visit" her privately, she chooses instead to live on his son's plantation. Harriet also decides for herself when she must leave her hiding places. She would rather risk her own life than place her family and friends in danger. Often Harriet's only choices are between two evils. She makes up her mind to live with poisonous snakes in a swamp and with biting insects in her grandmother's tiny attic. She prefers such torture to living in Dr. Flint's fine, but evil, house.

Harriet also takes control of her communication. She decides when to speak out, and when to remain silent. When "poor white bullies" search her grandmother's house, they grab a box of cash. Harriet protests politely, but firmly, "But now that you have searched that box, I will take it back, if you don't mind." When Dr. Flint bullies and provokes her, Harriet sometimes talks back to him. But sometimes she uses her silence to take charge of the situation. She tells her master only what she wants him to know, and sometimes she misleads him with lies. Her clever plan of having letters sent from the North keeps Dr. Flint from seeing that she is hiding right in his own town. Of course, Harriet keeps completely silent when Dr. Flint passes by her peephole on his way to the office. And she does not make a sound when her grandmother invites the sheriff and the slave hunter for Christmas dinner. When Mrs. Hobbs lets Harriet take Ellen if she agrees to bring her back within ten days, Harriet tells the reader that she carefully "avoided making any promises." Sometimes Harriet does not speak her thoughts aloud, but the reader can still, in a sense, hear her voice. For in writing her story, Harriet is free to express her true feelings and beliefs.

Harriet decides for herself what is right, and she always follows her own conscience. Although she writes that "Slavery deadens a person's sense of morality," Harriet holds onto her sense of right and wrong, even when it means defying the church, the law, and the traditional roles of women. Harriet sees through other people's phoniness. She criticizes hypocrites like Mrs. Flint, who goes to church on Sunday and then spits into the leftovers meant for her cook's children. Harriet also knows that many ministers do not "practice what they preach." Some even twist words in the Bible to keep slaves from becoming free. Harriet's beliefs about God are strong, yet very personal. After her mother, father, mistress, and friend die, Harriet says that her young heart "rebelled against God." And yet, she continues to keep her own faith—a faith that God loves people no matter what their skin color, and wants them all to be free.

Harriet also questions the laws of her country. Why should she be forced to be a prisoner in an attic, while Dr. Flint is free to abuse his slaves? What kind of justice is that? Although the law says that she is Emily Flint's "property," Harriet refuses to pay cash for the freedom that is rightly hers. Why should she obey laws that are so clearly unjust?

Finally, in writing *Incidents*, Harriet refuses to "pretty up" the truth about what she experienced, whether or not her story upsets readers. She chooses to keep her integrity, rather than give up her hard-won independence. Despite the terrible hardships she faced, Harriet Jacobs is never a helpless victim. She faces the realities of her life squarely, and she takes responsibility for her choices. In doing so, she finds an inner freedom—the freedom to be true to herself, even when she is forced to be a slave to others.